Reliability Management

An Overview

EQE International, *an ABS Group Company*

Government Institutes
Rockville, Maryland

04   03   02   01   00   5   4   3   2   1

ISBN 0-86587-671-1

Printed in the United State of America

Thank you for choosing EQE International's *Reliability Management: An Overview* as your system reliability resource

IF YOU ARE LOOKING FOR MORE HELP . . .

EQE International personnel have helped clients worldwide design, construct, operate, and maintain processes and systems to meet reliability, productivity, quality, and economic goals. Based on the three principles for achieving reliability excellence introduced in this book, our personnel follow a holistic, integrated approach to investigating and dealing with reliability problems. Such an approach helps ensure that not only the symptoms, but also the root causes of the problem are being properly addressed. EQE International can help you resolve reliability issues in any department or across your organization as whole, either by working directly with your personnel to solve the issues or through training your personnel in the application of tools and techniques based on the three principles.

EQE INTERNATIONAL TRAINING SERVICES

Drawing on our extensive field work experience, we teach a curriculum of reliability-related courses. Thousands of individuals from dozens of different industries are applying techniques learned from us at facilities around the world. We also customize courses to make them specific to a facility, company, or industry. Customized courses can range from 1 to 5 days in duration. Some of our most popular courses are listed below.

- Reliability Management
- Root Cause Analysis
- Preventing Human Error
- Reliability Centered Maintenance
- Reliability Focused Design
- Failure Modes and Effects Analysis
- Writing Effective Maintenance Procedures
- Business Interruption Risk Assessment
- Changing Workplace Culture

EQE INTERNATIONAL CONSULTING SERVICES

In addition to our extensive training curriculum, EQE International offers consulting services in all of the areas that our training programs cover. Our staff does more than just teach classes. They are out in the field applying what they teach to help you solve real problems. So, if you need help . . .

- identifying your most critical reliability problems
- performing root cause analysis
- implementing reliability centered maintenance
- assessing your business interruption risks
- calculating specific reliability metrics
- designing for reliability
- generating optimum maintenance and operating procedures
- preventing human errors, or
- decision support analysis

. . . EQE International can help. Use the form on the next page to contact us and find out how EQE International can help you solve your reliability problems.

CONTACT US FOR INFORMATION AND ASSISTANCE

If you would like a catalog of our complete line of courses or more information about how our analysis services could be used at your facility, contact EQE International.

- by phone at **1-865-966-5232**,
- by fax at **1-865-966-5287**,
- by e-mail at **info-jbfa@abs-jbfa.com**, or
- through the world wide web at **http://www.abs-jbfa.com**

You may also copy, complete, and fax the form below (or mail it to us at **EQE International, Inc., 1000 Technology Drive, Knoxville, TN, 37932-3353, USA**).

INFORMATION REQUEST FORM

__ Please send me your latest training catalog.

__ Please send me more information about your reliability management consulting and training services.

Name: _____

Title: _____

Company: _____

Address: _____

City: _____

State: _____

Zip: _____

Phone: _____

Fax: _____

E-mail: _____

Table of Contents

Introduction to *Reliability Management: An Overview*

This manual introduces you to the concepts of reliability management. The purpose of the handbook is to provide you with an overview of the tasks your organization needs to accomplish to achieve reliability excellence.

Improvements in reliability are usually driven by one basic premise: improvements in reliability performance have a positive effect on the company's financial performance. So the issues and language of reliability must be related to the issues and language of the financial world. Therefore, a portion of this handbook examines how reliability improvements can result in increased production revenues, decreased production expenses, and reductions in net asset values. All of these will result in improvements in the financial performance of the company.

Many organizations take too narrow a view when implementing reliability programs. They tend to focus on only a small portion of the organization: maintenance. This handbook takes a broader view. To achieve reliability excellence, all portions of the organization must work together. This includes not only the maintenance organization, but operations, engineering, procurement, stores, and all other organizations of the company. Without this coordinated, integrated effort, the organization will not realize all of the improvements that are possible.

Therefore, the concepts discussed in this handbook are based on the following broad principles for achieving reliability excellence.

Principle 1:   Reliability Management
Principle 2:   Proactive Analysis
Principle 3:   Root Cause Analysis

Implementing these three principles requires the coordinated efforts of all parts of the organization. These three principles are the basis for developing and implementing an effective reliability management program.

Implementation of an effective reliability improvement program will certainly have a positive effect on the financial performance of the organization, but it also has a positive effect on safety performance and on the attitude of the employees.

Implementation of an effective reliability improvement program is not easy. Any organizational change is difficult, and one that requires the unified efforts of all of the personnel is all the more difficult. But the rewards of performance improvements are worth the efforts.

Limitations of Liability

Acknowledgements

EQE International, Inc. thanks the many personnel who contributed to the development and ongoing revision of this handbook, particularly its primary authors, Randal L. Montgomery, Lee N. Vanden Heuvel, and David A. Walker. We also thank Leslie K. Adair, Rebekah Ellis, John A. Farquharson, and J. Rufus Gomez for reviewing this handbook. And we thank Jill M. Johnson, Paul M. Olsen, Robin M. Ragland, and Maleena L. Wright for their skill and craftsmanship in preparing this handbook. We are also grateful for the support and assistance of the rest of the staff at EQE International, Inc.

Chapter 1
Introduction to Reliability

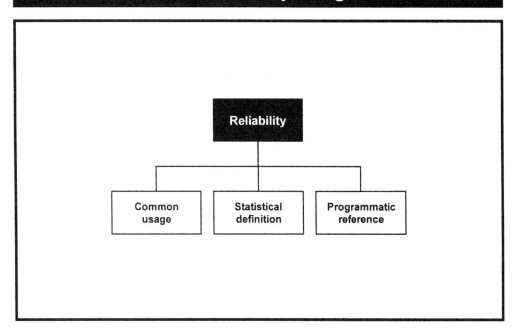

What Is Reliability?

Much like quality, reliability is a word that people use all the time without precisely understanding its meaning. The following are three closely related, but distinct, interpretations of the term reliability:

Common usage   Planned performance without loss of function

Statistical definition   Probability of experiencing no loss of function over a period of time under specific conditions

Programmatic reference A collection of planned activities (established through formal and informal management systems) that are effectively working together to prevent loss of system function

This handbook focuses on the programmatic aspects of reliability management, which encompass both the common and statistical aspects of reliability. For clarity, we will use the following conventions (or similar phrases) when discussing various aspects of reliability:

Performing reliably   Refers to the common usage of the word reliability

Reliability   Refers to the statistical definition of reliability

Managing reliability   Refers to the programmatic aspect of reliability

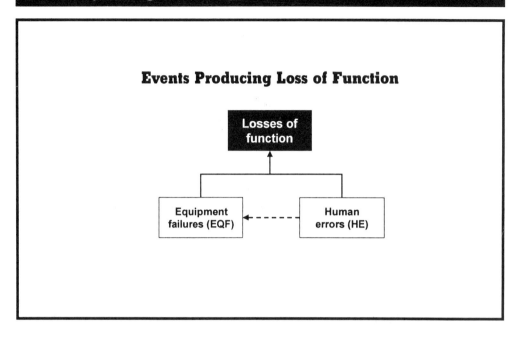

Events Producing Losses of Function

A specific loss of system function is caused by a combination of one or more equipment failures (EQF) and/or human errors (HE). (In fact, human errors are also the underlying causes of most equipment failures.) For each loss of system function, there are generally many combinations of events that can produce that performance problem.

Combinations of events producing a loss of function

- EQF #1
- EQF #2, EQF #3
- HE A, HE B
- EQF #4, HE C
- HE A, HE C, HE D
- Etc.

Example

A lighting system has a single power supply and two light bulbs in parallel. The entire circuit is protected by a single breaker and controlled by a single switch. The following is a list of events contributing to a lack of room lighting:

- Power supply fails off
- Wiring failure
- Circuit breaker fails open
- Switch fails open
- Operator inadvertently opens switch
- Light bulb #1 fails off; light bulb #2 fails off
- Operator incorrectly installs light bulb #1; operator incorrectly installs light bulb #2

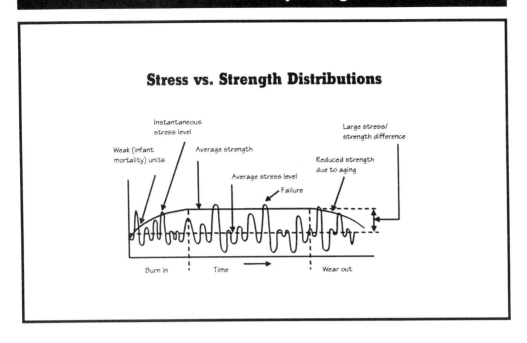

Equipment and Component Failures

Equipment life periods

An equipment failure is a state or condition in which a component no longer satisfies some aspect of its design intent.

Equipment failure occurs when the "stress" on the component exceeds the component's "stress resistance." (In this case, "stress" refers to some negative influence and "stress resistance" refers to the component's resistance to that influence.)

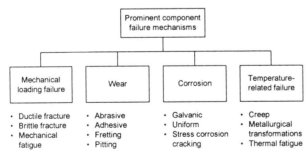

Typical frequency of mechanism of failure in industry

- Corrosion   (29%)
- Fatigue   (25%)
- Brittle fracture   (16%)
- Overload   (11%)
- High temperature corrosion   (7%)
- Environmentally assisted cracking   (6%)
- Creep   (3%)
- Wear, abrasion, erosion   (3%)

Causes of Component Failures

- **Faulty design**
- **Faulty material**
- **Improper fabrication**
- **Incorrect construction**
- **Misoperation**
- **Inadequate maintenance**

Causes of Component Failure

Component failures can be caused by mistakes that are made throughout the life cycle of a component. Often, the errors made early in the process must be addressed by operations and maintenance personnel.

Faulty design
- Incorrect equipment sizing
- Improper material specified
- Weld joints in regions of high stress
- Structural discontinuities, notches, etc.
- Etc.

Faulty material
- Material chemistry out of specification
- Improper heat treatment
- Etc.

Improper fabrication
- Improper materials used
- Improper welding
- Incorrect machining tolerance
- Improper stress relief
- Etc.

Incorrect construction
- Improper mounting
- Component misalignment
- Improper welding
- Bolts improperly torqued
- Use of incorrect cleaning fluids
- Etc.

Misoperation
- Improper start-up
- Operating outside safe design limits
- Severe service conditions
- Etc.

Inadequate maintenance
- Repairs performed incorrectly
- Unsuitable replacement parts
- Preventive maintenance not performed
- Etc.

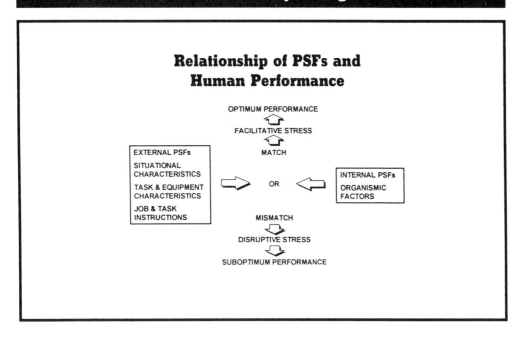

Relationship of PSFs and Human Performance

Human Errors

Human error is an intentional or unintentional action (or inaction) that is outside of the prescribed course of action. Human error is often the dominant contributor to system failures and is generally the underlying problem even when equipment failures play a significant role in system failures.

System failures resulting directly from human errors *

Missiles	20 to 53%
Nuclear weapons	28 to 82%
Electronic systems	23 to 45%
Aircraft	60 to 90%
Nuclear power	70 to 80%
Petrochemical	65 to 90%

* Adapted from Swain, *Human Reliability Analysis*, 1993

Human performance is strongly influenced by performance shaping factors (PSFs), which include the following:

External PSFs	Situational characteristics Task/equipment characteristics Job/task instructions
Stressor PSFs	Psychological stressors Physiological stressors
Internal PSFs	Organismic factors

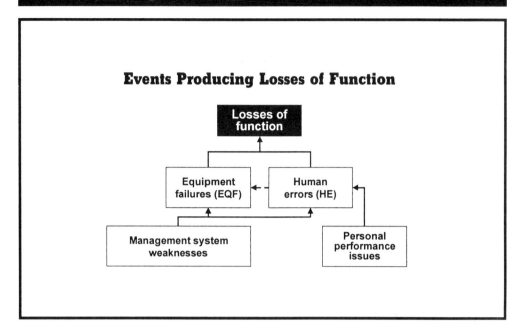

The Root Causes of Loss Events

Although equipment failures and human errors are the most direct causes of unreliable system performance, the underlying root causes of such problems are typically management system weaknesses.

Management systems are the mechanisms that are used to control:

(1) how equipment is designed, fabricated, operated, and maintained, and

(2) how personnel are trained, instructed, and supervised.

Weaknesses in these management systems (1) create vulnerabilities that allow equipment to fail and (2) create error-likely situations that increase the likelihood of human errors. Thus, these weaknesses are generally the true root causes of reliability problems.

Of course, management system weaknesses are not the only root causes of problems. Sometimes, personal performance is inadequate, regardless of the quality of management systems. A management system's perspective on root causes does not excuse or disregard individual personal performance issues.

Chapter 2

The Business Case for Reliability-related Improvements

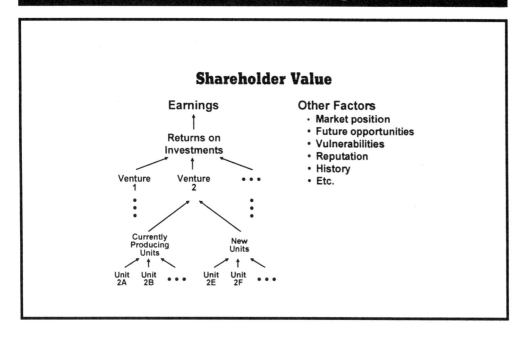

Shareholder Value

The Corporate Goal: Shareholder Value

The best place to begin talking about the business case implications of reliability performance improvements is in regard to the fundamental business driver for most organizations. Generating maximum **shareholder value** (or owner equity) is the key financial objective of any business entity. Even in not-for-profit and governmental organizations, generating maximum value for the associated stakeholders is a key objective.

Of course, generating maximum shareholder value is a complicated process that is dependent on many **factors** (such as those listed in the figure above). However, **earnings** (profits) produced by a business entity have historically proven to be one of the most important and most manageable factors affecting shareholder value. Most of the attention and effort of the executive management team within an organization is focused on identifying and managing all of these factors, especially earnings. Ultimately, success or failure of each activity within the organization is judged by how it contributes to shareholder value (most often through earnings).

To generate earnings, business entities must most effectively allocate scarce resources to **ventures** (types of business activities) that produce the greatest returns. Thus, the principal measure of success for most ventures within a business entity is the **return on the investments** in those ventures. (Of course, some other measures, such as the payback time, are also important for measuring and controlling financial success.) Many business entities involve themselves in a number of diverse business ventures, seeking the optimal balance of ventures with attractive returns on investments. Again, executive management teams have this primary responsibility in guiding their business entities for the shareholders. In deciding whether to commit resources to products, facilities, staff, programs, etc., they base their decisions on expected returns on investments. This consideration is especially important when these managers must seek outside sources of capital to fund ventures (loans, bonds, stock sales, etc.).

In industry, business ventures use production units to generate the returns that feed overall earnings. During any given performance period, revenues are generated by (1) **existing units** that continue to produce, and (2) **new units** that are brought on-line. The managers for the various business ventures (typically divisional staffs) must focus on returns on investments from all of their units. Their attention should be on managing all of the factors within their control/influence to ensure that these units meet the return on investment criteria necessary to achieve earnings goals (and subsequently shareholder value).

In turn, the responsibilities for controlling these factors that influence return on investment for particular units are delegated to those who design, build, manage, operate, and maintain individual units. This leads us to the all-important question, "What can these people really do to ensure an attractive return on investment from the units with which they have been entrusted?" As we will see, the influences on return on investment are many, and each branch of the organization has primary responsibility for some of these influences. But, for the purposes of this handbook, we will only explore how reliability-related issues affect returns on investments. Before we can answer the question above, we need to define a metric for measuring return on investment.

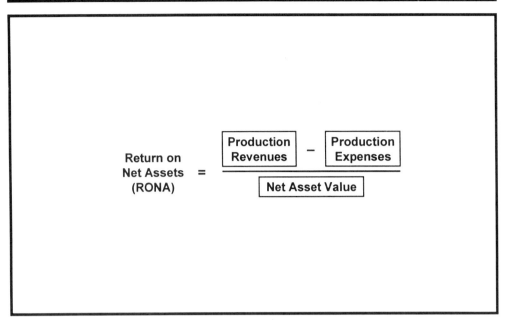

Return on Net Assets

There are many different types of measures for returns on investments; each has a slightly different flavor/meaning. Each business entity chooses measures that are most meaningful to it. Rather than trying to represent many different measures, we will explore one representative measure for the purposes of this manual. The measure that we will use is **return on net assets (RONA)**. Your organization may use somewhat different measures or a slightly different calculation of this measure.

The basic concept of RONA is expressed in the equation presented above. The key elements of the equation are the following:

- **Production revenues**. The total sales value of quality product sold over a defined period of time (often 1 month)
- **Production expenses**. The sum of all noncapital investment expenses used to produce the products sold over the same defined period of time
- **Net asset value**. The current value of all of the assets invested in the production of the products during the production period

RONA expectations vary widely across industry segments. Of course, the goal is to maximize production revenues while minimizing both the production expenses and the value of the assets committed to the production operation.

Now, let us look at which RONA variables are most affected by reliability-related issues.

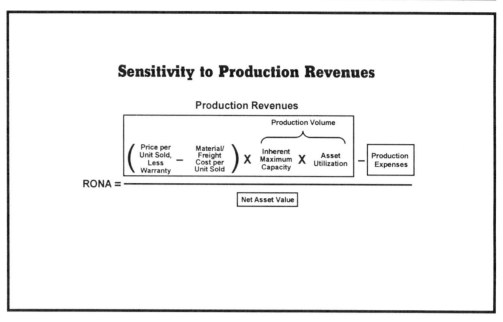

Sensitivity to Production Revenues

Assuming that we can sell all of the product that we can produce, increasing production revenue (with little or no increase in production expenses and assets invested) can produce a substantial increase in RONA. And, even small increases in RONA typically translate into sizable earnings increases for business ventures.

Production revenue is the marginal value on each unit of production (price per unit sold minus the material/freight costs per unit sold) times the production volume (i.e., the number of units sold). Generally speaking, product price and material/freight costs are set by the market. (However, creative design of the product/process and strategic supplier/distributor alliances can certainly affect these variables.) The variable most affected by reliability-related issues is the production volume.

Production volume for a manufacturing unit is determined by two factors:

- **Inherent capacity of the unit.** The maximum production possible from the unit assuming that the unit operates without interruption over some period of time (i.e., 100% utilization)

- **Actual asset utilization for the unit.** The fraction of the inherent capacity that is being realized (range from 0 to 1.0, or 0% to 100%)

The following figure illustrates how a relatively modest change in asset utilization can produce a substantial change in RONA.

	Production Revenue				Production Expenses	Net Assets	RONA (annual)
	Price/ Unit	M&H Cost/Unit	Inherent Capacity	Asset Utilization			
Baseline	$10	$5	22,000/month	65%	$70,000/month	$1M	1.8%
Improved	NC	NC	NC	70%	NC	NC	8.4%

NC: No Change

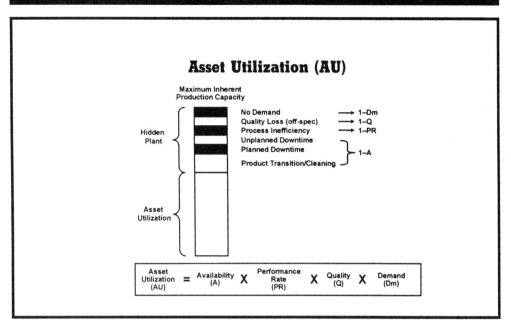

Asset Utilization (AU)

The concept of asset utilization deserves some further consideration. The figure above illustrates the concept of asset utilization and provides an equation for calculating asset utilization for a manufacturing process.

The inputs into the asset utilization equation are the following:

- **Availability**. A number ranging from 0 to 1 representing the average uptime percentage for a unit over a period. Various companies include/exclude different classes of downtime from this calculation to suit their measurement needs. The most conservative (and recommended) measurement accounts for all types of downtime, except downtime because of lack of demand (as will be addressed shortly).

- **Performance rate**. A number ranging from 0 to 1 representing the average percentage of the maximum production rate (i.e., the inherent capacity) being achieved over a period. (Some companies base this calculation on the maximum theoretical rate, while others use a maximum demonstrated rate.)

- **Quality**. A number ranging from 0 to 1 representing the average percentage of product conforming to specifications over a period. Generally, this number includes "rework" that subsequently meets specifications. (Of course, this rework adversely affects the performance rate, as described above, and introduces additional costs that are not addressed in asset utilization calculations. These will affect production costs, which is addressed later in this section.)

- **Demand**. A number ranging from 0 to 1 representing the average fraction of available production time (typically 24 hours a day, 7 days a week) for which there is demand for unit production. The only downtime associated with this factor is downtime during which the unit could have been producing, but was idle because of lack of demand. No penalty is subtracted if idle periods coincide with productive, planned maintenance periods that have already been addressed in the availability number.

Another popular metric used in conjunction with production volume is overall equipment effectiveness (OEE). OEE is the product of availability, performance rate, and quality. OEE does not include a penalty for idle periods resulting from a lack of demand.

$$\text{OEE} = \text{Availability (A)} * \text{Performance Rate (PR)} * \text{Quality (Q)} = \frac{\text{Asset Utilization (AU)}}{\text{Demand (Dm)}}$$

The following table summarizes a few asset utilization/OEE calculations for a few manufacturing units and for what many people would consider "world-class" performance.

Metric	Case 1	Case 2	"World-class" Performance
Availability	0.8	0.9	>0.95
Performance Rate	0.8	.9	>0.95
Quality	0.9	0.9	>0.95
Demand	0.24 (1 shift, 5 days)	0.9	~1.0
Asset Utilization	0.14	0.66	>0.85*
OEE	0.58	0.73	>0.85

*Some organizations view world-class asset utilization as 90%+. Of course, the achievability of different levels of performance varies from industry to industry.

Example production volume metric calculations

The following page provides a template worksheet for calculating these production volume-related metrics.

Estimate of OEE and Asset Utilization for a Machine or Process

Machine/Process:

1	**Estimate Availability**		
1a	Estimate the fraction of scheduled production time lost to planned maintenance (i.e., time that would have been spent producing if planned maintenance had not been performed)		
1b	Estimate the fraction of scheduled production time lost to unplanned maintenance (i.e., shutdowns or delays for repairs)		
1c	Estimate the fraction of scheduled production time lost to other sources of forced outages (e.g., loss of utilities)		
1d	Estimate the fraction of scheduled production time lost to product transitions and system cleaning		
1e	Add fractions recorded for lines 1a, 1b, 1c, and 1d		
1f	Subtract the fraction recorded in 1e from 1.0		
2	**Estimate Performance Rate** Estimate the fraction of the maximum credible production rate (i.e., inherent capacity) for the machine/process that is being achieved		
3	**Estimate Quality**		
3a	Estimate the fraction of production that does not meet specifications and must be reworked or scrapped		
3b	Estimate the fraction of production that is reworked (effectively reducing the performance rate estimated above)		
3c	Subtract the fraction recorded for 3b from that recorded for 3a		
3d	Subtract the fraction recorded for 3c from 1.0		
4	**Estimate OEE** Multiply 1e, 2, and 3d		
5	**Estimate Demand** Estimate the fraction of possible production time (24 hrs, 7 days) that the machine/process is idle because of no demand (do not include idle time that is productively used for planned maintenance, as long as this period of time is accounted for in line 1a)		
6	**Estimate Asset Utilization** Multiply 4 and 5		

Key Points for Bolstering RONA Through Higher Production Volume

- Provide adequate inherent production capacity
- Minimize production transition and system cleaning/preparation time
- Minimize planned maintenance downtime
- Minimize unplanned maintenance downtime
- Minimize process inefficiencies
- Minimize quality defects
- Minimize idle periods for machines

Achieve Higher Production Volume

Provide adequate inherent production capacity (accounting for expected asset utilization)

- Design to meet current and reasonable future demands
- Avoid excess capacity that may unnecessarily increase the investment in assets and complicate the process

Minimize production transition and system cleaning/preparation time through creative design and efficient operating practices

- Design systems for easy cleaning
- Design systems for rapid changeover from one product to another
- Use effective production planning and scheduling systems

Minimize planned maintenance downtime

- Eliminate the need for maintenance to the extent possible
- Define rational planned maintenance tasks with appropriate frequencies based on risks
- Design for improved maintainability/monitoring of equipment and systems
- Provide for timely access/delivery of tools and spare parts for maintenance work
- Develop highly skilled technicians to efficiently perform tasks
- Use effective work planning and scheduling systems
- Design in backups/installed spares to allow maintenance without affecting system operability

Minimize unplanned maintenance downtime

- Design equipment and systems to minimize equipment failure rates, human mistakes, and vulnerability to external events/influences that lead to process downtime
- Manage equipment procurement, shipping, and storage/handling to prevent defects that lead to process downtime when the equipment is operated
- Design for improved constructability of equipment and systems to minimize startup delays
- Design for improved maintainability of equipment and systems to minimize detection/repair times
- Provide for timely access/delivery of tools and spare parts for construction/ installation work
- Provide for timely access/delivery of tools and spare parts for maintenance work
- Develop highly skilled technicians to efficiently perform problem detection and diagnosis, perform installation/repair tasks, and to prevent maintenance/construction errors that lead to subsequent failures
- Use effective work planning and scheduling systems
- Assign appropriate types of maintenance to equipment and perform these activities at the proper frequency
- Avoid designs that appear to have short component repair/reset times, but actually experience long outages for restart cycles, decontamination/ cleaning, etc.

Minimize process inefficiencies by identifying/eliminating bottle-necks and other constraints that keep a system from sustaining maximum production rates

- Identify system bottlenecks and expand capacity through improved design

Minimize quality defects (off-specification product) that reduce productive process output (and also increase production expenses)

- Design equipment and systems to minimize equipment failure rates, human mistakes, and vulnerability to external events/influences that lead to off-specification products
- Manage raw material procurement, shipping, and storage/handling to prevent defects that lead to off-specification products
- Develop highly skilled technicians to prevent (1) operations mistakes that lead to quality defects and (2) maintenance/construction errors that lead to subsequent failures with associated quality defects

Minimize idle periods for machines

- Improve marketing/sales of product
- Improve product to better meet the customer's needs
- Reduce production costs so that product cost to customer can be reduced, thus increasing demand

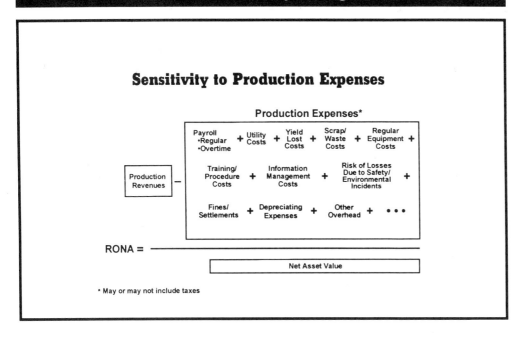

Sensitivity to Production Expenses

Of course, increasing production value is not the only way to increase RONA. Reducing production expenses has the same effect as increasing production value. In fact, this is often where many organizations begin trying to improve performance. Unfortunately, they often fail to account for potentially adverse impacts that some cost-cutting measures may have on production revenues and/or net asset values. Some examples of misguided cost-cutting measures that actually decrease RONA include the following:

- **Arbitrarily reducing operating/maintenance staffs**. Fewer operators and technicians may reduce payroll expenses, but these savings can easily be more than offset by increases in other (less visible) and usually delayed expenses, as well as decreases in production value (primarily from lower asset utilization). The following are some of the earmarks of this type of mistake:
  - greater process inefficiencies, product transition times, and defect rates because of understaffing in the operations department
  - increased downtime, increased number of unplanned failures, equipment replacement costs, and utility consumption costs because of understaffing in the predictive/preventive maintenance area

- **Reducing training and procedure writing**. Training and procedure writing can be sizable expenses, but the true costs of not developing a highly skilled staff can be enormous. Engineering, operating, and maintenance staffs who are not equipped to implement reliability-enhancing strategies directly increase other expenses and limit asset utilization potential.

- **Choosing not to invest in information management tools**. Modern information management systems (like a computerized maintenance management system [CMMS] or a distributed control system [DCS]) are expensive and require cultural change in an organization, which is also expensive. But without such tools, the factors affecting RONA cannot be effectively understood, much less managed.

- **Cutting back on safety and environmental program activities**. Programs for preventing safety and environmental incidents (such as process safety management) are not cheap to operate. Sometimes economic pressures tempt organizations to cut back on some of these programs because the events that the programs are designed to prevent are already "relatively rare." These events are "relatively rare" in part because of the efforts the company has made in safety and environmental program efforts. One significant event can introduce equipment loss, legal settlement, and regulatory fine expenses that dwarf most of the other production expenses. In addition, improvements in safety and environmental programs generally have a positive effect on the reliability performance of an organization.

Although there certainly are some pitfalls, many productive approaches to reducing production expenses do exist. The following figure illustrates how a relatively modest, but appropriate, change in production expenses can produce substantial changes in RONA.

	Production Revenues	Production Expenses	Net Assets	RONA (annual)
Baseline	$71,500/month	$70,000/month	$1M	1.8%
Improved	NC	$65,000/month	NC	7.8%

- Reduce maintenance by introducing autonomous maintenance
- Focus on energy consumption

- Resell scrap/waste for salvage value
- Establish new supplier alliances

Key Points for Bolstering RONA Through Lower Production Expenses

- Control payroll expenses
- Minimize utility costs
- Minimize yield loss costs
- Reduce scrap/waste costs
- Reduce equipment/parts replacement costs
- Control training and procedure writing costs
- Improve information management
- Manage risks efficiently
- Minimize other overhead expenses

Lowering Production Expenses

Control payroll expenses

- Reduce maintenance/operations overtime pay by eliminating equipment failures that lead to emergency repairs and associated unplanned downtime
- Prioritize the types of repairs and planned maintenance work that should be performed on overtime
- Improve maintainability/operability of systems to reduce labor demands
- Eliminate unnecessary maintenance tasks and optimize the intervals for necessary inspections/tests
- Balance equipment care responsibilities by implementing autonomous maintenance through the operations/maintenance departments
- Focus staff on core competencies and contract for other services (if appropriate)
- Base the type and frequency of maintenance activities for a component on a reliability analysis of the process
- Reduce overstaffing (if it truly exists)

Minimize utility costs

- Reduce waste by eliminating equipment failures and human mistakes that consume utility resources (e.g., steam trap leaks)
- Explore utility supplier alliances to improve utility costs
- Monitor for inefficiencies in utility consumption and investigate more efficient usages
- Eliminate utility system failures that reduce the availability and reliability of production processes

---

Minimize yield loss costs

- Optimize use of materials through design of experiments of processing conditions
- Reduce yield losses by eliminating equipment failure and human mistakes that create losses

Reduce scrap/waste costs

- Reduce scrap/waste costs by eliminating equipment failures, human mistakes, and vulnerabilities to external events/influences that lead to off-specification products
- Manage raw material procurement, shipping, and storage/handling to prevent defects that lead to off-specification products
- Develop highly skilled technicians to prevent maintenance/construction errors that lead to subsequent failures

Reduce equipment/parts replacement costs

- Reduce costs by eliminating equipment failures, especially ancillary damage
- Reduce unnecessary replacements/rebuilds of equipment through condition monitoring and life extension (when appropriate)
- Explore vendor alliances to improve equipment/part costs
- Manage equipment/part procurement, shipping, and storage/handling to prevent defects that lead to equipment/part failures in service
- Develop highly skilled technicians to prevent maintenance/construction errors that lead to subsequent failures
- Consider elimination of low volume, low profit products to reduce the number of spare parts required

Control training and procedure writing costs

- Focus training and procedure writing on the most critical areas
- Use just-in-time training (when appropriate) to improve effectiveness and avoid unnecessary training for many who will never perform certain tasks or need certain knowledge
- Use computer-based training and internet/intranet training modules to deliver some training to field personnel during their on-shift discretionary time (rather than set aside days or even overtime hours)
- Avoid unnecessary training and procedure writing recommendations by focusing on the true root causes of problems that develop

Improve information management

- Invest wisely in information management tools to reduce other expenses, facilitate improvement in asset utilization, and understand/reduce invested asset values
- Avoid overcomplicating information collection/management by only collecting information that truly affects decision-making processes within the company (i.e., not collecting data just to collect data)

Manage risks efficiently

- Assess risks in a measurable way and apply risk management resources (insurance, failure prevention efforts, contingency plans, etc.) in proportion to the assessed risks (i.e., balancing risks with the costs of managing the risks)

- Integrate risk management program activities with other management systems to make them more efficient (combining hazard analyses and reliability-centered maintenance [RCM] studies; integrating reliability, quality, safety/health, and environmental programs; etc.)

Minimize other overhead expenses

- Address the other types of expenses (such as taxes) that also reduce the RONA that an organization realizes

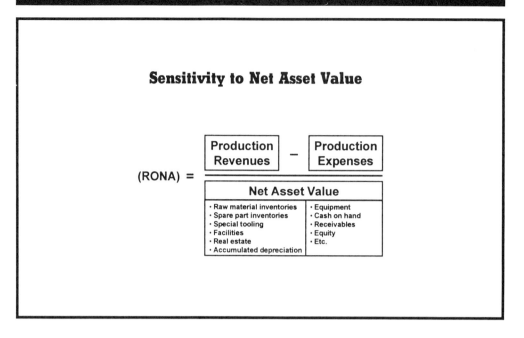

Sensitivity to Net Asset Value

A third way of increasing RONA is to reduce the net asset value invested in the process. Many organizations find that they have far too many financial resources tied up in their ventures. If these resources could be freed, they could be invested in other ventures that would produce greater earnings (and subsequently greater shareholder value) for the corporation. Some of the most common pitfalls in this area are the following:

• Excessive inventories of raw materials, equipment/spare parts, and product that equate to millions of unproductive dollars sitting in warehouses. In addition, there are costs associated with the warehouse itself and all the utilities needed to operate it.

• Notable excess capacity and expensive redundancy in processes because of unreliable equipment and error-likely situations

• Large/diverse tool cribs and spare parts storage because of a lack of standardization and use of common tools/parts whenever possible

• Poor cash flow management, particularly failing to minimize accounts receivable

The following figure illustrates how a change in net asset value through appropriate business improvements can produce changes in RONA. Note that small changes in net asset value do not produce as substantial an impact on RONA as small changes in production value or production expense. However, the reduction in asset values also can reduce many types of expenses (rent, maintenance costs, taxes, insurance, etc.). And, more importantly, these actions free up additional capital that can be used elsewhere to produce earnings. For example, the $150,000 in available assets could be invested in a new venture that could produce 15% to 25% RONA.

	Production Revenues	Production Expenses	Net Assets	RONA (annual)
Baseline	$71,500/month	$70,000/month	$1M	1.8%
Improved	NC	NC	$850,000	2.1%

- Eliminate unnecessary spare parts and raw material inventories

- Sell excess equipment
- Reduce accounts receivable

Key Points for Bolstering RONA Through Lower Net Assets

- Raw material inventories
- Equipment
- Equipment/spare parts inventories
- Special tooling
- Facilities/real estate
- Financial assets
- Other assets

Lowering Net Assets

Raw material inventories

- Explore just-in-time delivery of raw materials to minimize inventories and warehousing requirements
- Reduce "contingency" inventory by improving production planning and scheduling

Equipment

- Avoid unwarranted excess capacity
- Avoid nonpertinent capabilities/features
- Avoid unnecessary redundancy in process designs
- Use "novel" equipment or complexity only when absolutely necessary (because it is generally more expensive and less reliable)

Equipment/spare parts inventories

- Reduce the need for replacement equipment and spare parts by eliminating equipment failures
- Explore just-in-time delivery of replacement equipment and spare parts for planned maintenance work to minimize inventories
- Purge inventories of obsolete/outdated/unneeded equipment and spare parts
- Explore equipment/part supplier alliances (including rapid delivery methods, consignment bins, etc.) to minimize inventories
- Optimize stocking of critical equipment/spare parts based on risks of not stocking the parts (and have contingency plans when a "no-stock" decision is made)
- Standardize equipment to reduce inventory of unique items

Special tooling

- Minimize tooling requirements by standardizing (to the extent possible) the tools needed
- Avoid overstocking tools (especially those that are rarely used and could be effectively rented/leased on demand)

Facilities/real estate

- Account for future reasonable growth expectations, but avoid excess commitment of resources to unneeded facility capabilities and real estate for future expansion
- Invest the resources in facilities/real estate necessary to minimize other expenses (especially losses that could result if a major incident such as a fire/explosion occurred)

Financial assets

- Manage cash on hand, receivables, equity, etc., to minimize asset value, but assure positive cash flow
- Take advantage of depreciated asset values

Other assets

Of course, there are other types of assets that must also be managed effectively.

Synergistic Effects

	Production Revenues	Production Expenses	Net Assets	RONA (annual)
Baseline	$71,500/month	$70,000/month	$1M	1.8%
Improved	$77,000/month	$65,000/month	$850,000	16.9%

Based on changes described earlier

The improved case could generate roughly a 50% increase in shareholder value!

Synergistic Effects of Improvement Actions on RONA

The synergistic effect of taking a set of actions that simultaneously increase production value, decrease production expenses, and reduce the investment in assets is startling. For example, if all of the improved cases from the previous examples are combined together, the RONA improvement is amazing.

Impact on shareholder value

Assuming that this was the only unit that a company operated and the company had 1,000,000 shares of stock, we can roughly estimate the increase in shareholder value. In the baseline case, the annual earnings for the company would have been $18,000, or $0.018/share. If the price of a share of stock were based on a price-to-earnings ratio of 5 plus the value of the assets, each share of stock would have been worth $1.09. With all of the improvements implemented, the annual earnings would have jumped to $144,000, or $0.144/share. Additionally, the company would have $850,000 in assets invested in the unit, plus $150,000 in freed assets to pursue other ventures. The value of each share of stock would then be $1.72. This is an increase of approximately 60% in shareholder value. (Of course, many simplifying assumptions have been made about the company, taxes, time value of money, etc., in these demonstration calculations, but the message is perfectly clear.)

This is the business case for any reliability-related (or virtually any other) improvement action that is undertaken. Now you understand the variables that will directly translate into shareholder value, which is a term that gets maximum attention in most companies. Who pays attention? Everyone!

- **Shareholders.** It is their money and their future. They will vote for actions that protect and enhance their investments.

- **The Board of Directors.** The shareholders appoint these people to oversee their investments. Their primary purpose is to preserve and enhance shareholder value.

- **Executive Management.** The Board of Directors hires these people to guide the company in a way to maximize shareholder value, while limiting risks. Their compensation is generally a strong function of shareholder value, generally paid in large bonuses and stock options.

- **Management.** They define the specific strategies and tactics for implementing the vision/direction set forth by executive management. Their compensation and their retirement benefits (as well as their employment stability and career progression) are strongly dependent on shareholder value, generally including bonuses and stock options.

- **Employees.** They implement the business plans issued by management. Their compensation and retirement benefits (and employment stability) are increasingly tied to shareholder value criteria. In fact, in most companies these days, they are shareholders themselves.

- **Communities.** The communities in which companies operate are also concerned about shareholder values because strong companies contribute most to the community through taxes, stable employment, donations, etc.

In short, messages related to shareholder value are heard. And, managers or employees will seldom make informed decisions choosing paths that ultimately degrade shareholder value.

Chapter 3
System Performance Pyramid

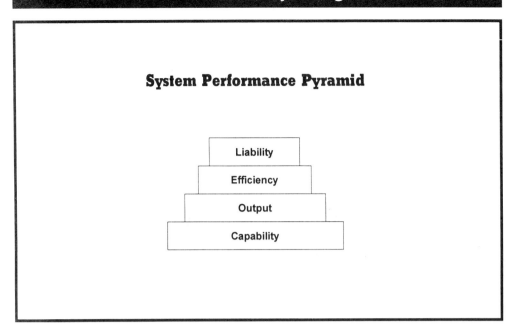

There are four fundamental measures for judging system performance:

Capability

A measure of ability to produce the desired product/effect (i.e., conformance with assessed needs)

Output

A measure of production

Efficiency

A comparative measure of resources consumed to outputs produced

Liability

A measure of risk exposure (economic, safety/health, environmental, regulatory, legal, etc.)

Unreliable system performance and use of resources for ensuring reliable system performance can have significant impacts on each of these measures.

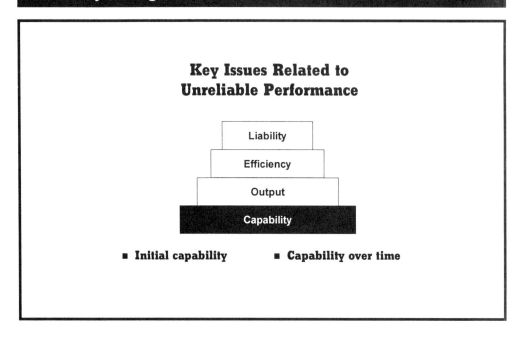

Key Issues Related to Unreliable Performance

- Liability
- Efficiency
- Output
- Capability

■ **Initial capability**   ■ **Capability over time**

Most issues related to product or process capability are independent of reliability program issues. Product or process features are planned to meet defined needs, and appropriate specifications are developed to ensure that the resulting product or process meets the defined needs. Capability is essentially a measure of how accurately the product or process meets those defined needs (i.e., a measure of the appropriateness of the specifications and conformance to those specifications).

However, the ability of a system to perform reliably does affect capability in the following ways:

Initial capability

The basic design of a system or product establishes how reliably it can perform its intended functions. A system with inherent design/manufacturing deficiencies (e.g., inadequate tolerances and/or lack of control of critical parameters) may not be able to produce results consistently enough to be judged capable, even if no failures/errors occur. Unreliable performance caused by an inherently unstable system (e.g., too much variability) certainly influences basic judgments about the capability of the system.

Capability over time

Even with routine maintenance and repairs, most products and processes reach a point at which their performance degrades below established specifications. At this point, which is strongly influenced by past failure history, the system may be judged to be incapable.

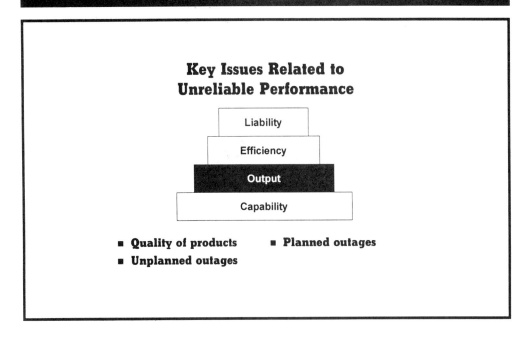

Key Issues Related to Unreliable Performance

- **Quality of products**
- **Unplanned outages**
- **Planned outages**

Output is the number of units of production (items, pounds, etc.) provided by a unit. For specified conditions, a system has a theoretical maximum capacity. This maximum capacity can be achieved only if (1) every unit of production meets established specifications, (2) the unit suffers no failures that interrupt operations, and (3) the unit does not remain idle during times in which it could be producing.

The output of a system can be calculated as follows:

Output = Capacity * Overall Equipment Effectiveness (OEE)

The ability of a system to perform reliably affects output in the following ways:

Quality of products

Unreliable system performance may cause out-of-specification production, even though the system continues to operate at its rated load. Out-of-specification products reduce actual output below maximum attainable levels.

Unplanned outages

Unreliable system performance may interrupt operations, which yields actual output below maximum attainable levels.

Planned outages

Planned outages, including efforts to prevent unreliable system performance (e.g., turnarounds for preventive maintenance and needed component repairs/retrofits/retooling), reduce actual output below maximum attainable levels.

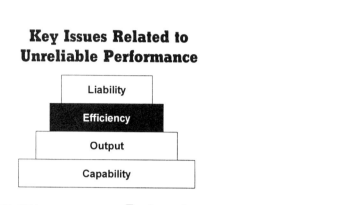

**Key Issues Related to
Unreliable Performance**

- **Human resource
  consumption**
- **Material consumption**
- **Equipment
  consumption**
- **Utility consumption**

Efficiency is the ratio of productive system outputs to inputs. Controlling the level of inputs necessary to produce outputs is the key to measurement of efficiency. For industrial products and processes, inputs include a wide range of human, material, equipment, and energy resources. For specified conditions, a system has an optimum efficiency point that minimizes waste.

The ability of a system to perform reliably affects efficiency in the following ways:

Human resource consumption

Unreliable system performance requires extra human resources for response, diagnosis, and correction of problems (e.g., unplanned maintenance work to repair equipment failures).

Material consumption

Unreliable system performance wastes materials used in producing off-specification products resulting from process upsets (e.g., a bad batch of chemical product that must be incinerated).

Equipment consumption

Unreliable system performance destroys capital equipment and wastes consumable materials of construction (replacing failed motors, pump seals, sensing equipment, bearings, etc.).

Utility consumption

Unreliable system performance wastes energy through inefficient use of utility resources (excessive steam usage through defective steam traps, excessive nitrogen consumption through leaking vents on tanks, inappropriate control of power factors, etc.).

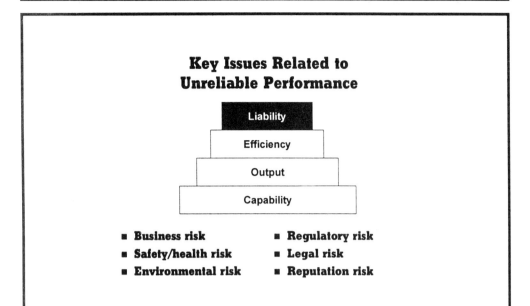

Key Issues Related to Unreliable Performance

- Liability
- Efficiency
- Output
- Capability

- Business risk
- Safety/health risk
- Environmental risk
- Regulatory risk
- Legal risk
- Reputation risk

Liability (as a measure of system performance) is a measure of risk exposure beyond the direct costs of performance problems. The risk is the potential for further adverse consequences that often lead to greater costs than the direct costs of unreliable performance. The following are various types of risk exposure where unreliable system performance can cause significant problems:

Business

Unreliable system performance can cause substantial, and sometimes lasting, effects on business conditions for a company (e.g., reduced market share caused by product scarcity, poor consumer response because of quality problems, loss of contracts as a supplier because of supply interruptions and/or quality problems, etc.).

Safety/health

Unreliable system performance can lead to incidents that endanger the safety/health of employees, contractors, and/or the public (e.g., releases of hazardous materials or energy).

Environmental

Unreliable system performance can lead to incidents that release contaminants into the environment (e.g., contamination/exceedances of permitted discharges and/or other accidental releases).

Regulatory

Incidents caused by unreliable system performance can also lead to substantial penalties (fines, operating prohibitions, shutdowns, etc.) from regulatory agencies.

Legal

Safety/health and environmental incidents can also lead to lawsuits that seek substantial awards for damages suffered as a result of unreliable system performance. Furthermore, violation of contractual terms between companies as a result of unreliable system performance can also result in substantial awards for damages.

Reputation

Publicized safety/health, environmental, regulatory, and quality problems resulting from unreliable system performance can cause negative public opinion that can severely impact a company's sales.

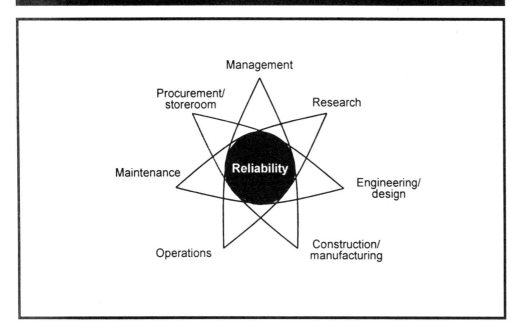

World-class Performance

World-class reliability performance requires contributions from each organization within a company. The following provide some of the typical roles that various organizations within a company need to provide to achieve the company's reliability goals.

Research

Provide advanced technologies and methodologies to increase the inherent reliability of the new and existing systems. Assist in making and transferring these technologies and methods to production scale.

Design

Design equipment incorporating the technologies and methods provided by research. Consult with construction, operations, maintenance, procurement, and others to ensure the needs of these groups are designed into the system.

Construction/manufacturing

Adhere to specifications outlined in the design documentation. When these specifications can't be met, work with the design organization to modify them.

Operations

Operate the equipment within the control limits. Work with other groups to ensure the system is designed and maintained to meet operational needs.

Maintenance

Perform tasks to predict system failures, prevent system failures, and restore equipment operability. Perform these tasks to maintain system capability at the level of the original design.

Procurement/storeroom

Provide adequate levels of spares to address the requirements of maintenance and operations. Ensure that spares are appropriately maintained and parts can be located when needed.

Management

Develop and implement management systems that reward actions that are consistant with the long-term goals of the organization, including reliability.

The next section provides additional details and examples of the roles of these organizations in achieving reliability excellence.

Chapter 4

A Life Cycle Approach to Performing Reliability Analysis

A Life Cycle Approach to Performing Reliability Analysis

- **Research**
- **Design**
  - ◆ conceptual
  - ◆ preliminary
  - ◆ detailed
- **Fabrication/ construction/ manufacturing**

- **Operation**
  - ◆ startup
  - ◆ ongoing
- **Decommissioning**

Research

Analysis focuses on assessing inherent reliability of certain technologies. Primarily interested in technical models ("physics of failure") of how failures occur over time, number of demands, number of cycles, etc. Also interested in key parameters that must be controlled in design, manufacturing, and operation to translate research technology into viable applications.

Design

Analysis focuses on ensuring that the selected configuration/operating strategy will provide the necessary reliability-related performance to meet overall performance goals/objectives established from customer needs. Keenly interested in identifying "weak links" and opportunities for improvements in components and systems.

Conceptual phase

Analysis focuses on determining how overall performance goals/objectives translate to goals/objectives for individual systems. Assessment (at a high level) of whether required reliability-related performance is realistically achievable and what modifications/improvements would be necessary to meet overall goals/objectives. Comparison of various design concepts to determine which option(s) deserves further development based on a variety of factors, including project risk and expected life cycle costs (such as the cost of unreliability and its prevention).

Preliminary phase

Analysis focuses on determining how individual system goals/objectives translate to component goals/objectives. Assessment (at a more detailed level) of whether required reliability-related performance is realistically achievable and what modifications/improvements would be necessary to meet system goals/objectives. Optimization of expected system performance characteristics based on a number of factors (including costs, quality of products, reliability-related characteristics, etc.).

Detailed phase

Analysis focuses on ensuring that component selection and configuration allows systems to meet individual component goals/objectives. Assessment (at a component level) of whether required reliability-related performance is realistically achievable and what modifications/improvements would be necessary to meet component goals/objectives. Optimization of component selection based on a number of factors (including costs, quality of products, reliability-related characteristics, etc.). Also interested in:

1) critical parameters for reliable fabrication/construction/ manufacturing,
2) important operating limits and startup criteria,
3) appropriate preventive/predictive maintenance tasks, and
4) necessary spare parts/materials stores.

Fabrication/Construction/Manufacturing

Analysis focuses on ensuring that established specifications have been satisfied and identifying any special fabrication/construction/manufacturing issues not identified during design that could affect reliability-related performance. Assessment of the potential significance of any identified field nonconformances, as well as any proposed changes during fabrication/ construction/manufacturing.

Operation

Analysis focuses on optimization of operating/maintenance/supply strategies while achieving reliability-related goals/objectives.

Startup

Analysis focuses on ensuring that operating/maintenance strategies (including plans, procedures, and training) promote realization of inherent reliability and are optimized based on a variety of factors (including costs, quality of products, reliability-related characteristics, etc.).

Ongoing

Analysis focuses on ensuring that:
1) changes (planned, unplanned, and unintentional) do not significantly affect reliability-related performance, and
2) operating/maintenance strategies remain optimized based on a variety of factors (including costs, quality of products, reliability-related characteristics, etc.), especially in light of data that will become available over years of operation.

Decommissioning

Analysis focuses on liability issues associated with decommissioning (e.g., safety, health, and environmental risks) and what actions to take to control those risks to acceptable levels.

Reliability Analysis Applications for Senior Management Issues

Examples

- ◆ Improving the bottom line by reducing downtime
- ◆ Assessing business risks and developing contingency plans
- ◆ Comparing competing project funding alternatives

Reliability Analysis Applications for Senior Management Issues

Improving the bottom line by reducing downtime

A new plant manager took the job with clear direction from corporate headquarters to improve the economic performance of the consistently poorly performing plant. Immediately after taking the position, the plant manager formed a team to evaluate key metrics of reliability-related performance and assess how changes in these metrics could improve overall plant economic performance. The plant manager found that many aspects of plant operations were not as bad as expected (although room for improvement existed), but did find that the plant suffered from excessive downtime (low average availability). The plant manager commissioned a high-level reliability analysis of the plant (using multidisciplinary teams of experienced personnel), which has five distinct manufacturing processes. The analysis confirmed the low availability of the plant (70 to 75% uptime for the processes) and generated more than 30 recommendations for improvement. These recommendations included changes in equipment and equipment configuration, development of critical operating limits and associated procedures/training, and projects to investigate new technologies for process control. The team prioritized the recommendations and worked with management to assign responsibilities for resolution. Within 6 months, half of the recommendations had been resolved, and uptime for the processes had significantly increased (80 to 85% uptime for each process). Within a year, only a few recommendations remained unresolved (i.e., those addressing long-term improvement projects) and uptime had further increased (85 to 90%). This turnaround saved the plant from being shut down, and the plant became one of the top five plants in the corporation.

Assessing business risks and developing contingency plans

A corporation has recently consolidated production operations that used to occur at three locations across the country into one new, centrally located production facility. Because all production will hinge on the success of this facility, the Board of Directors is concerned about the risk of business interruption and how well management has developed plans for dealing with potential contingency situations (major equipment problems, catastrophic events at the plant, supply/distribution interruptions, labor disputes, natural disasters, etc.). The Board hired an outside consultant to assess the risks of production interruptions of longer than two weeks and to make recommendations for effectively managing those risks. The Board also asked management to develop formal plans for dealing with each type of potential contingency to minimize losses. The business risk analysis generated a number of recommendations for both prevention of and response to problems that could occur. The contingency plan outlined actions and roles/responsibilities for dealing with those potential problems.

Comparing competing project funding alternatives

At budget time each year, the executive council for a company reviews proposed projects to determine which of the many good ideas will be funded. Because of some past problems, the council has begun to focus on total life cycle costs of projects in relation to their benefits. One of the council's most significant concerns associated with life cycle costs is "the cost of unreliability" over time (in contrast to initial costs alone). The council now requires rough estimates of total life cycle costs (including costs strongly influenced by unreliable performance) for all projects submitted for funding. This information need forces proposal managers to perform high-level reliability assessments of their concepts/designs even before the project is fully funded. The council believes they are making better project funding choices (i.e., more attractive total life cycle cost to potential benefit ratios) even though they frequently choose projects with fewer benefits or greater initial costs over other projects.

**Reliability Analysis Applications for
Research and Development Issues**

Example

♦ **Developing failure
   models as part of
   technology
   development**

Reliability Analysis Applications for Research and Development Issues

Developing failure models as part of technology development

Although new technologies developed by the research and development (R&D) department have helped lead to many new products over the years, the R&D manager has undergone some criticism from design/engineering personnel because the reliability of applications using such new technology has not been well-understood. The R&D manager has begun addressing these concerns in two ways:

1) having researchers develop models of reliability performance for new technologies they develop (e.g., fatigue life models for new composite materials, failure rate models for new components), and

2) launching special projects to investigate unique reliability problems (e.g., lubrication strategies for bearings/seals, unrecognized failure mechanisms).

Reliability Analysis Applications for Design/Engineering Issues

Examples

- ◆ Assessing instrumented system (interlock) protections for code/standard compliance
- ◆ Evaluating redundancy options for cost-effective reliability improvement
- ◆ Assessing human factors issues in control systems
- ◆ Allocating reliability-related goals/objectives to systems, subsystems, and components

Reliability Analysis Applications for Design/ Engineering Issues

Assessing instrumented system (interlock) protections for code/standard compliance

The engineering manager for a company became aware of recent interpretations by the ASME Boiler and Pressure Vessel Code committee allowing the use of highly reliable, instrumented systems for pressure relief protection as an alternative to traditional pressure relief valves. The manager assigned a project engineer to complete a preliminary design of such an instrumented system as an alternative to potentially troublesome/expensive relief valves on future designs. Then, the manager commissioned a reliability analysis of the system to:

1) compare expected performance with traditional relief valve arrangements, and

2) identify weaknesses (including common-cause failures) that could be improved.

The analysis led to correction of one fundamental flaw in the design, as well as several other dependability improvements. Additionally, the analysis demonstrated that the system is expected to perform more reliably than the traditional relief protection devices.

Evaluating redundancy options for cost-effective reliability improvement

A project engineer faced a dilemma in trying to meet control system specifications with strict safety and operability requirements. The individual components of the system could not perform reliably enough to meet the stringent requirements; thus, the designer was faced with using equipment redundancy to meet the requirements. The engineer performed a reliability analysis to evaluate which redundancy options (redundant components, redundant systems, multiple redundancies, etc.) would best meet the requirements. The analysis indicated that 2-out-of-3 voting logic systems were the best alternative. Additionally, the analysis identified three important common-cause failure potentials that could defeat the planned redundancy. Recommendations were generated to minimize/eliminate potential problems.

Assessing human factors issues in control systems

A project engineer was responsible for the design of a control panel for a highly instrumented, complex process. When a preliminary layout of the control system was complete, the engineer decided to perform a human factors analysis of the layout to identify possible improvements. The review (involving teams of people expected to actually use the control panel) identified numerous improvements in location, labeling, audible/visible feedback, etc.

Allocating reliability-related goals/objectives to systems, subsystems, and components

A project team for a new product used benchmarking results of expected competition and direct customer input to establish overall reliability-related performance goals for the product. Then, the team developed reliability block diagrams of the major system/subsystem/component configurations to understand the range of possibly acceptable performance at each level. Using this information and estimates of costs for achieving various levels of component/subsystem/system performance, the team "optimized" the design to achieve the desired overall performance goals at minimal cost.

Reliability Analysis Applications for Construction/Manufacturing Issues

Example

♦ Evaluating the risk/reliability significance of identified non-conformances

Reliability Analysis Applications for Construction/Manufacturing Issues

Evaluating the risk/reliability significance of identified nonconformances

The construction manager for a new process was faced with a difficult situation when the wrong piping material was used to fabricate a long line between existing processes and the new process. Rather than immediately replacing the piping, the manager initiated a small analysis to assess the significance of the nonconformance and determine what (if any) corrective actions should be taken. The analysis determined that the material was suitable for the application as long as periodic inspections would be performed more frequently than had originally been planned.

**Reliability Analysis Applications
for Operations Issues**

Examples
- ◆ Identifying and evaluating critical procedures to minimize the potential for human error
- ◆ Evaluating the risk/reliability significance of proposed changes/upgrades

Reliability Analysis Applications for Operations Issues

Identifying and evaluating critical procedures to minimize the potential for human error

An operations manager recognized that over the next three years 75% of the operations staff would retire. Recognizing that so many new operators in the plant could significantly increase the number of operating mistakes and related safety/reliability problems, the manager commissioned an effort to upgrade the plant's procedures. The intent was two-fold:

1) to provide clear instructions for new operators and

2) to capture the wisdom of the very experienced members of the staff before they retire.

As part of this procedure project, the manager also asked that the procedures be systematically analyzed to identify and protect against potential operator mistakes. Numerous enhancements and corrections of error-likely situations were made in the procedures.

Evaluating the risk/reliability significance of proposed changes/upgrades

A process engineer wanted to use a new type of controller in a process. The operations manager initiated a small analysis to assess the significance of the proposed change on operations and related maintenance. The analysis found that the inherent error rate of the proposed controller was much higher than existing controllers in the plant. The proposal was rejected even though the new controller may have been able to provide some advanced control capability.

**Reliability Analysis Applications
for Maintenance Issues**

Examples

- ◆ Assessing maintainability of components/systems
- ◆ Preserving system function through reliability-based maintenance task selection
- ◆ Life extension of a major equipment item
- ◆ Improving procedure quality

Reliability Analysis Applications for Maintenance Issues

Assessing maintainability of components/systems

Customers had been complaining about the amount of time necessary for expensive service personnel to repair a manufacturer's office products. The maintenance costs were becoming an issue that was beginning to affect sales (especially to repeat customers). The product manager for the flagship product line initiated an analysis to:

(1) identify where the most maintenance hours were being spent and

(2) identify what improvements could be made to reduce time spent on those issues.

The analysis and resulting improvement actions reduced the number of service calls by 75%.

Preserving system function through reliability-based maintenance task selection

In an effort to optimize maintenance operations, a maintenance manager commissioned analyses of processes to identify the most important contributors to unreliable system performance and select appropriate maintenance tasks to preserve system function. The analyses considered various planned maintenance tasks (e.g., corrective, preventive, predictive, proactive) as options for addressing potential problems. Also, the analysis considered how changes in the equipment design and configuration could eliminate/reduce the need for maintenance tasks. The project led to significant reductions in maintenance costs by ensuring that each task addressed dominant failure modes that cause loss of system function and by making maintenance more proactive and less reactive (i.e., more planned versus unplanned).

Life extension of a major equipment item

A nondestructive examination of a pressure vessel indicated some signs of cracking in the vessel wall. The maintenance manager and engineering manager initiated a reliability analysis to determine how much longer the pressure vessel could remain in service. Based on engineering knowledge and failure models, the analysis determined that the vessel could reasonably be expected to remain in service for the next five to ten years, but that more frequent inspection would be necessary to monitor the situation for any acceleration in crack growth.

Improving procedure quality

After multiple failures following product switches in which a critical bonding roll was changed, the production team leader requested that a root cause analysis be performed. The results showed that maintenance procedures for preparing and installing the rolls were not being followed and were not up-to-date. As a result, the maintenance team leader requested a thorough review of 12 critical maintenance procedures, including the bonding roll changeout procedure. These reviews produced the addition of 49 new steps, the deletion of 32 incorrect or unneeded steps, the inclusion of multiple key warnings and notes, and significant knowledge transfer between operations, engineering, and maintenance on why each step within the procedures is so important.

Reliability Analysis Applications for Procurement/Storeroom Issues

Example

◆ Establishing spare part/material inventories and delivery plans based on risk/reliability significance of components

Reliability Analysis Applications for Procurement/ Storeroom Issues

Establishing spare part/material inventories and delivery plans based on risk/reliability significance of components

A small plant had oscillated between excessive inventories of spare parts/ materials (leading to excessive costs) and inadequate inventories (adversely affecting plant performance). Under fire from plant management, a procurement manager initiated a review of reliability-related data to optimize the quantities of spare parts/materials. Where failures are infrequent, the analysis tried to forecast when such failures might be expected so that plans for responding to the failures could be made (e.g., scheduling replacement of major equipment items).

Chapter 5
Three Principles for Achieving Reliability Excellence

Three Principles for Achieving Reliability Excellence

- **Principle 1: Reliability management**
  - ◆ holistic, integrated management practices
- **Principle 2: Proactive analysis**
  - ◆ proactive analysis of potential reliability-related problems
- **Principle 3: Root cause analysis**
  - ◆ solution of reliability-related problems through root cause analysis

---

Principle 1: Holistic, integrated management practices

Because management system weaknesses are typically the underlying causes of system performance problems, proactive development and implementation of holistic (i.e., addressing all key reliability control mechanisms) management systems are fundamental keys to preventing future reliability problems.

Principle 2: Proactive analysis of potential reliability-related problems

Analyzing systems to identify, prioritize, and react to potential reliability-related problems (i.e., combinations of equipment failures and human errors leading to system performance problems) is another key to preventing future reliability-related problems. These types of analyses are traditionally cornerstones of reliability programs.

Principle 3: Solution of reliability-related problems through root cause analysis

Systematic analyses and strong management systems cannot completely eliminate the possibility of reliability-related problems. Root cause analysis identifies the underlying reasons why problems occur and corrects the root causes so that the same problem and other problems (similar and/or seemingly unrelated) with shared root causes do not occur in the future.

These principles form a practical and effective foundation for reliability excellence when applied in conjunction with each organization within your company.

Principle 1: Holistic, integrated management practices

Commitment and accountability	Teamwork	Technology usage	Contractor fitness for duty	Reliability-related analysis
Community outreach	Equipment stewardship	Procedures/ instructions	Conformance testing	Root cause analysis
Employee fitness for duty	Training/ proficiency testing	Management of change	Contingency planning	Measurement/ improvement

Elements of Reliability Management

The following are some of the most common elements of successful management systems for proactively preventing system performance problems and improving the overall reliability of your processes:

Organizational

- Commitment and accountability
- Teamwork
- Community outreach

People-oriented

- Employee fitness for duty
- Contractor fitness for duty
- Procedures/instructions
- Training/proficiency testing

Equipment-oriented

- Technology usage
- Equipment stewardship

Analytical

- Reliability-related analysis
- Conformance testing
- Management of change
- Root cause analysis
- Contingency planning
- Measurement/improvement

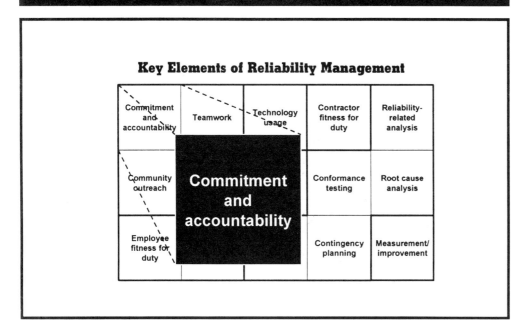

Key Elements of Reliability Management

Commitment and Accountability

The success of reliability management depends on a sincere management commitment that integrates reliability goals into overall performance plans and appraisals. In the most successful programs, reliability leadership occurs at every level of management. Management at all levels is accountable for meeting system reliability goals.

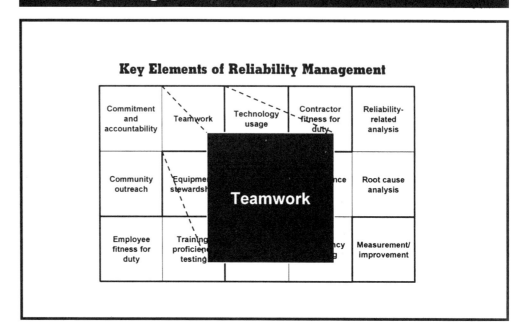

Key Elements of Reliability Management

Teamwork

Most organizations achieving world-class reliability performance use some type of team concept in work groups. Cooperative work among team members in each branch and level of the organization is important for achieving (and sometimes setting) the reliability goals that management expects. Teamwork among individual team members and between teams is critical for operating an effective and efficient reliability program.

Key Elements of Reliability Management

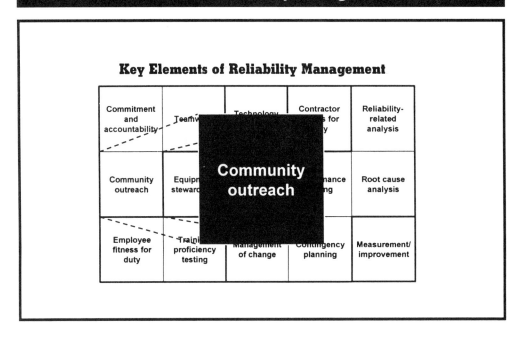

Commitment and accountability	Teamwork	Technology	Contractor s for y	Reliability-related analysis
Community outreach	Equipment stewardship	**Community outreach**	nance ng	Root cause analysis
Employee fitness for duty	Training proficiency testing	Management of change	Contingency planning	Measurement/improvement

Community Outreach

Although less critical than many of the other elements in reliability programs, community outreach can provide a positive relationship between a facility and surrounding communities. This relationship can:

1) lay the groundwork for community acceptance of plant expansion/reliability improvement projects and

2) help minimize negative community opinion that could lead to extended production outages after an incident.

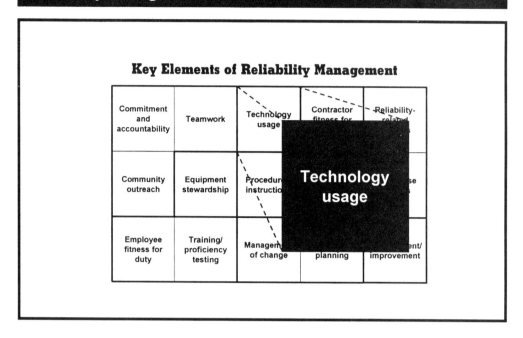

Key Elements of Reliability Management

Technology Usage

The inherent potential of a system to perform reliably is strongly influenced by the technology employed in the system. Most systems achieving world-class performance make use of modern, proven technology appropriate for the application. The most "advanced" or "sophisticated" technology may not (and frequently does not) provide the most reliable performance.

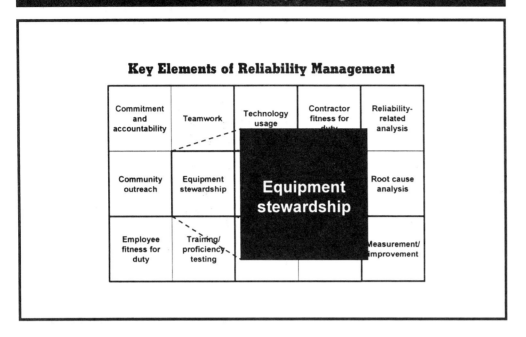

Equipment Stewardship

Because equipment failures play a key role in unreliable system performance, a focus on equipment monitoring/care is a prominent element of virtually all reliability programs. The best of these programs focus extensively on preventing failures from occurring through a variety of preventive, predictive, proactive, and failure finding tasks that are effectively planned to maximize the benefits (i.e., preserving system performance) of resources allocated to those tasks. However, because the possibility of equipment failures cannot be completely eliminated from even the most successful programs, equipment stewardship also includes reactive measures for correcting equipment failures in a reliable manner. The graphic below outlines the different types of maintenance tasks. The goal is to move to planned activities and away from unplanned reactive maintenance.

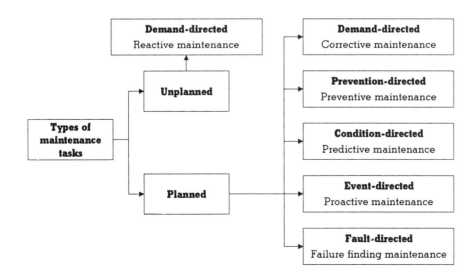

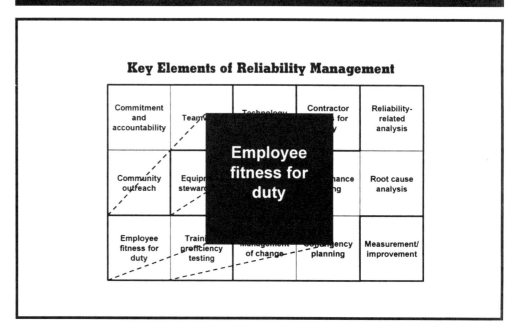

Key Elements of Reliability Management

Commitment and accountability	Team...	Technology	Contractor ... for	Reliability-related analysis
Community outreach	Equip... stewar...	Employee fitness for duty	...nance ...g	Root cause analysis
Employee fitness for duty	Train... proficiency testing	Management of change	...gency planning	Measurement/ improvement

Employee Fitness for Duty

Reliability program activities are based on assumptions of certain basic competencies and/or experience among people who will perform various types of tasks. Procedures and training are developed/implemented based on these assumptions. To help ensure that the procedures and training can reasonably be expected to control loss exposure, many reliability programs include activities for ensuring employee fitness for duty.

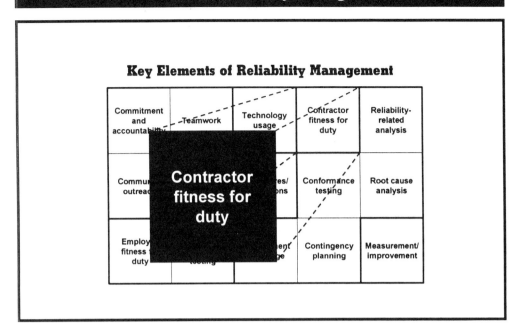

Key Elements of Reliability Management

Commitment and accountability	Teamwork	Technology usage	Contractor fitness for duty	Reliability-related analysis
Commu... outrea...	Contractor fitness for duty	...es/ ...ns	Conformance testing	Root cause analysis
Employ... fitness ... duty		...ent ...ge	Contingency planning	Measurement/ improvement

Contractor Fitness for Duty

Many facilities use contract employees to accomplish special projects (e.g., new installations and major renovations) and some routine tasks. Like direct employees, these contract employees must be fit to perform the tasks they are assigned. However, because a company does not have direct control of contract employees, the management system for ensuring contractor fitness for duty is different from the one for ensuring direct employee fitness for duty.

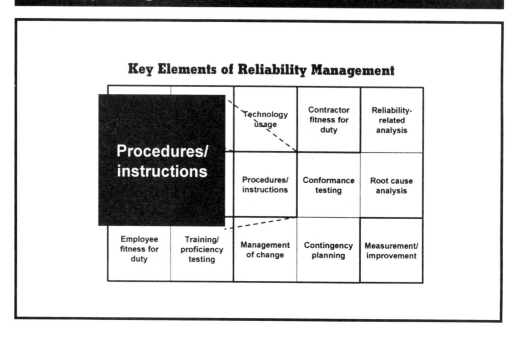

Key Elements of Reliability Management

		Technology usage	Contractor fitness for duty	Reliability-related analysis
Procedures/ instructions		Procedures/ instructions	Conformance testing	Root cause analysis
Employee fitness for duty	Training/ proficiency testing	Management of change	Contingency planning	Measurement/ improvement

Procedures/Instructions

Procedures/instructions are key elements for ensuring reliable performance of people. Procedures/instructions come in many varieties, such as task descriptions (e.g., operating and maintenance procedures), more general guidelines (e.g., design guidelines), and broad policy/program descriptions (e.g., safe work practices). Procedures define the approved (or at least preferred) method of performing activities to minimize loss exposure risks. Various companies use procedures with widely varying styles and levels of detail because of various company cultures, regulatory situations, applications, approaches to training, etc.

Key Elements of Reliability Management

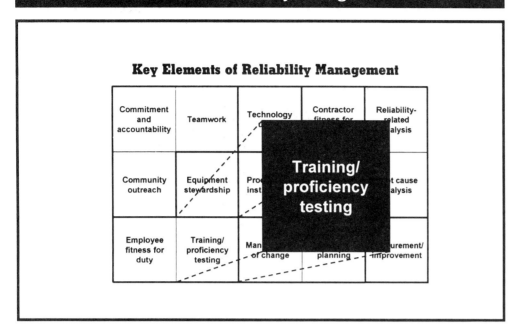

Commitment and accountability	Teamwork	Technology	Contractor fitness for	Reliability-related alysis
Community outreach	Equipment stewardship	Pro inst	Training/ proficiency testing	t cause alysis
Employee fitness for duty	Training/ proficiency testing	Man of change	planning	urement/ improvement

Training/Proficiency Testing

Training is a key element of any reliability or other loss prevention system. Almost no industrial companies develop procedures/instructions and design systems that the average person off of the street can reliably operate with no formalized training. (Consumer products are perhaps an exception to this statement.) The level of formal training required at any level is highly dependent on:

1) the level of detail in procedures/instructions,

2) how well human factors issues have been addressed in system design, and

3) the fundamental knowledge, skill, and aptitude requirements that constitute basic fitness for duty for specific positions.

Verification that personnel have understood the training is another key aspect of successful training programs.

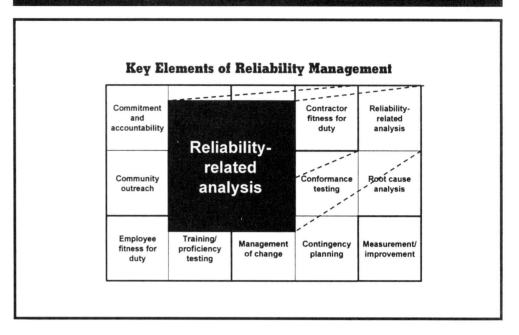

Key Elements of Reliability Management

Commitment and accountability	Reliability-related analysis		Contractor fitness for duty	Reliability-related analysis
Community outreach			Conformance testing	Root cause analysis
Employee fitness for duty	Training/proficiency testing	Management of change	Contingency planning	Measurement/improvement

Reliability-related Analysis

Proactive systems analyses are Principle 2 activities aimed at understanding:

1) how a system can perform unreliably,

2) how significant potential reliability-related problems may be, and

3) what actions can be taken to more effectively control loss exposure risks.

Proactive systems analyses are frequently the cornerstones of reliability programs. The different types of analyses that can be performed (and when they are most applicable) are described in this section.

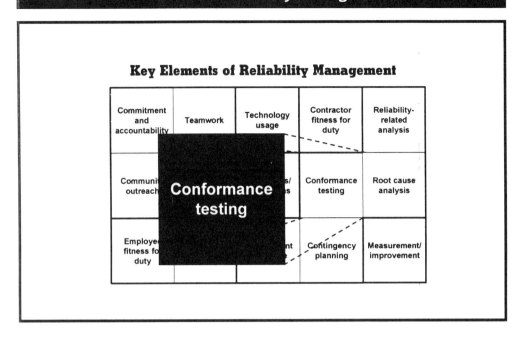

Key Elements of Reliability Management

Conformance Testing

Conformance testing ensures that systems and their products adhere to established specifications. To accomplish this, conformance testing addresses how well:

1) equipment designs/configurations meet established needs,

2) actual equipment conforms with design specifications, and

3) construction/maintenance activities keep equipment in conformance with specifications.

Additionally, conformance testing also addresses how well system products conform to established product specifications (i.e., traditional quality assurance tasks).

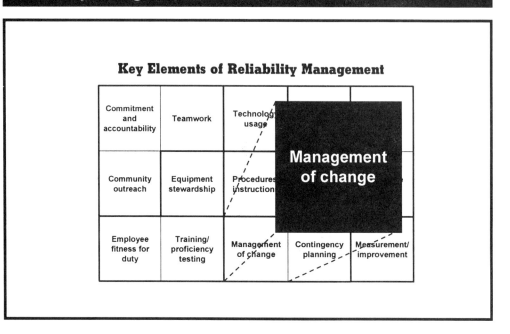

Key Elements of Reliability Management

Commitment and accountability	Teamwork	Technology usage	
Community outreach	Equipment stewardship	Procedures instruction	**Management of change**
Employee fitness for duty	Training/ proficiency testing	Management of change	Contingency planning	Measurement/ improvement

Management of Change

Inappropriate or unrecognized change in equipment, personnel, operations/ maintenance strategies, process materials, programs/policies, etc., is a leading cause of unreliable system performance. Management of change (sometimes referred to as configuration management) is a process for ensuring that changes are identified, reviewed, and appropriately approved/ rejected. This process also includes communication of changes to those whose work is potentially affected by the change, as well as documentation of changes.

Key Elements of Reliability Management

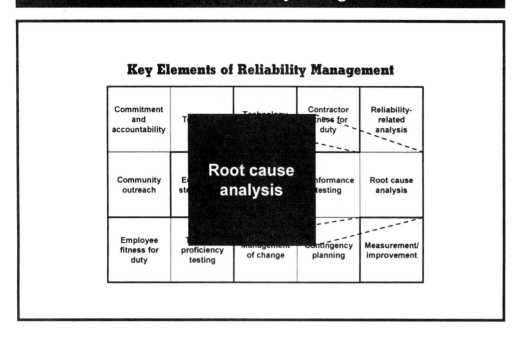

Commitment and accountability	T...	Technology	Contractor ...ness for duty	Reliability-related analysis
Community outreach	E... st...	**Root cause analysis**	...formance testing	Root cause analysis
Employee fitness for duty	...proficiency testing	...Management of change	...ntingency planning	Measurement/ improvement

Root Cause Analysis

Although the goal of a reliability program (or other loss prevention system) is to prevent undesirable events, such programs cannot completely eliminate the risk of problems occurring. When undesirable events occur, an effective program takes the opportunity to learn as much as possible from the event to prevent the same or other related failures in the future. This process is called root cause analysis. Root cause analysis focuses on identifying the underlying causes of problems (typically management system weaknesses), not just the symptoms that are apparent as equipment failures and human errors. In addition to investigating actual loss events, the most effective programs also investigate events that could reasonably have resulted in losses (often referred to as "near misses"). Broadly interpreted, root cause analysis includes equipment failure analysis and human error analysis.

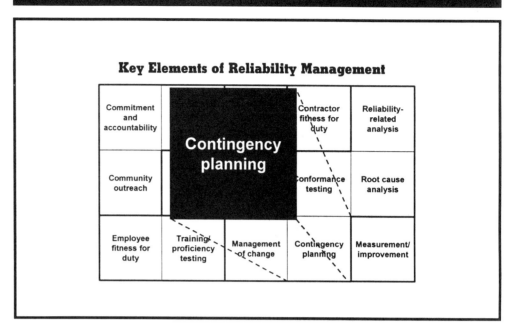

Key Elements of Reliability Management

Commitment and accountability	**Contingency planning**	Contractor fitness for duty	Reliability-related analysis
Community outreach		Conformance testing	Root cause analysis
Employee fitness for duty	Training/ proficiency testing	Management of change / Contingency planning	Measurement/ improvement

Contingency Planning

Many types of occurrences can have adverse effects on system performance. These occurrences include equipment failures, human errors, and external influences such as extreme phenomenological events (storms, extreme temperatures, and earthquakes), supply/distribution interruptions, labor problems, major accidents at nearby plants/processes, etc. Although many steps may be taken to prevent occurrences, planned responses for the various possible occurrences help restore system performance promptly (perhaps even before any significant loss occurs).

Key Elements of Reliability Management

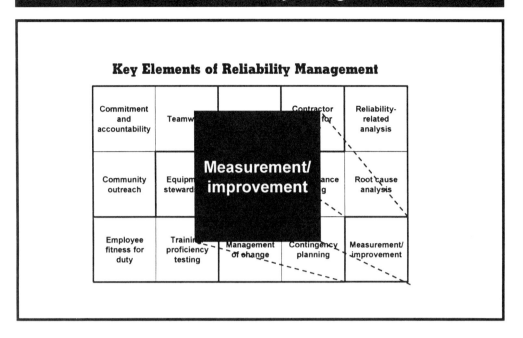

Measurement/Improvement

Measurement and continuous improvement are critical elements of effective reliability programs. Measurement of system performance (including measurement of factors related to reliability) allows comparisons with goals/objectives and identification of the areas in which improvements would be most helpful. The most beneficial measurement systems use both direct measurements (i.e., direct measurements of the desired system characteristics such as reliability, availability, etc.) and indirect measurements (i.e., leading indicators of how performance may change in the near future). In addition, effective measurement systems also include direct evaluations of reliability program elements to identify gaps in program design, development, and/or implementation. Effective measurement creates the opportunity for continuous improvement in pursuit of world-class performance.

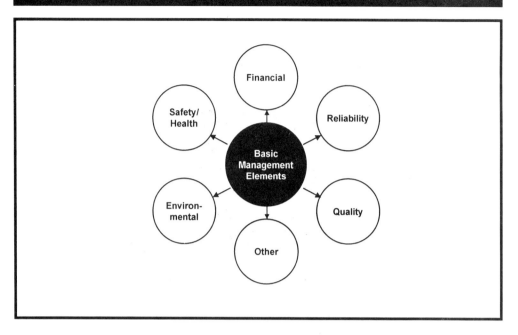

Integration with Other Management Programs

Most companies have many different types of management systems in use. Often, these management systems overlap (and sometimes conflict), which tends to cause inefficiency and poor implementation unless these overlaps have been well planned. The following are a few of the more prominent management programs that have activities similar to those found in a reliability program:

- Safety/risk management program — includes programs in industrial hygiene, traditional safety, process safety management, risk management, loss prevention, etc.

- Quality management program — includes programs such ISO 9000, etc.

- Financial management program — includes programs for compensation, procurement, acquisition, income, etc.

- Environmental management program — includes programs for fugitive emissions, hazardous waste, permitting, ISO 14000, etc.

Other programs have common elements shared with reliability programs.

Principle 2: Proactive Analysis

- **Screening analysis tools**
- **Broadly applicable, detailed analysis tools**
- **Narrowly focused, detailed analysis tools**

Reliability Principle 2, the proactive analysis of potential reliability problems, requires us to identify problems before they occur. This allows us to identify the required design, installation, operation, and maintenance strategies needed to ensure high reliability in our systems. A number of different analysis tools are available. Selecting the proper tool is dependent on many things, including the overall purpose of the analysis and the scope of the analysis. Commonly used tools can be divided into the three general categories discussed below.

Screening Analysis Tools

Used for high-level analyses intended to:

(1) provide a general characterization of expected performance, and

(2) identify the most significant areas of interest for further evaluation

Often generates some effective recommendations for improvement, but seldom at a detailed level

Example tools:

- Parts count analysis
- Pareto analysis
- Facility risk review (FRR)
- Relative ranking

Broadly Applicable, Detailed Analysis Tools

Used for more detailed analysis of complete systems that have been determined to be potentially important in some regard

Example tools:

- Checklist analysis
- Human factors checklist analysis
- What-if analysis
- Hazard and operability (HAZOP) analysis
- Worker and instruction safety evaluation (WISE) analysis
- Failure modes and effects analysis (FMEA)
- Single minute exchange of dies (SMED) analysis
- Fault tree analysis (FTA)
- Event tree analysis (ETA)
- Block diagram analysis

Narrowly Focused, Detailed Analysis Tools

Used for detailed analysis of specific items/issues/mechanisms that have been determined to be potentially important in some regard

Example tools

- Weibull analysis
- Markov analysis
- Simulation modeling
- Human reliability analysis (HRA)
- Common cause failure analysis (CCFA)
- Software failure analysis
- Physics-of-failure modeling

The following table summarizes the key characteristics of these methodologies. The pages that follow provide overviews of each of these methodologies.

Summary of Key Characteristics for Some Widely Recognized Analysis Techniques

Reliability Analysis Technique	Analysis Type		Types of Results				Types of Systems	Level of Effort/ Complexity	Level of Training for Analysts and Analysis Teams
	Deductive	Inductive	Qualitative Problem Descriptions	Quantitative Reliability Results	Relative Importance of Problem Contributors	Recommendations			
Parts Count Analysis	**See note			✓	✓	✓	All (especially simple electrical and/or mechanical systems)	Low	Low to Medium
Pareto Analysis	**See note		✓	✓	✓	✓	All	Low	Low
FRR		✓	✓	✓	✓	✓	All (primarily at the system/facility level)	Medium	Medium
Relative Ranking	**See note			✓	✓	✓	All (primarily chemical systems)	Low to Medium	Low to Medium
Checklist Analysis		✓	✓			✓	All	Low to Medium	Low
Human Factors Checklist Analysis		✓	✓			✓	All	Low to Medium	Low to Medium
What-if Analysis		✓	✓			✓	All	Medium	Low to Medium
What-if/ Checklist Analysis		✓	✓			✓	All	Medium	Low to Medium
HAZOP* Analysis		✓	✓			✓	Process systems (especially fluid and thermal systems) Sequential operations and procedures	Medium to High	Medium
WSE* Analysis		✓	✓			✓	Process systems (especially fluid and thermal systems) Sequential operations and procedures	Medium to High	Medium
FMEA*		✓	✓	✓	✓	✓	All (especially mechanical and electrical systems)	Medium to High	Medium
SMED*	**See note		✓	✓	✓	✓	All (primarily changeout and maintenance applications)	Low	Low
FTA*			✓	✓	✓	✓	All	High	Medium to High
ETA		✓	✓	✓	✓	✓	All	High	Medium to High

Summary of Key Characteristics for Some Widely Recognized Analysis Techniques (cont.)

Reliability Analysis Technique	Analysis Type		Types of Results				Types of Systems	Level of Effort/ Complexity	Level of Training for Analysts and Analysis Teams
	Deductive	Inductive	Qualitative Problem Descriptions	Quantitative Reliability Results	Relative Importance of Problem Contributors	Recommendations			
Block Diagram Analysis	✓	✓	✓	✓	✓	✓	All	Medium to High	Medium
Weibull Analysis	**See note		✓	✓	✓		Mainly mechanical components	Medium to High	Medium
Simulation Modeling/ Markov Analysis**			✓	✓	✓	✓	All	High	High
Human Error Analysis*		✓	✓	✓	✓	✓	Sequential operations and procedures	High	Medium to High
CCFA*	✓		✓	✓	✓	✓	All	Medium to High	Medium to High
Software Failure Analysis	✓	✓				✓	Software systems	Medium to High	Medium to High
Physics of Failure	**See note						All	High	High

* CCFA – Common cause failure analysis
ETA – Event tree analysis
FMEA – Failure modes and effects analysis
FRR – Facility risk review
FTA – Fault tree analysis
HAZOP – Hazard and operability analysis
SMED – Single minute exchange of dies
WISE – Worker and instruction safety evaluation

** Note: This technique does not typically demonstrate strong deductive or inductive characteristics.

Screening Analysis

Broadly Applicable Detailed Analysis

Narrowly Focused Detailed Analysis

Parts Count Analysis

Failure rate of component 1 (λ_1)

$+$ Failure rate of component 2 (λ_2)

$+$ Failure rate of component 3 (λ_3)

$+$ Failure rate of component 4 (λ_4)

$\bullet$

$\bullet$

$\bullet$

$=$ System Failure Rate (Λ)

$$\Lambda = \sum_{i=1}^{N} \lambda_i \qquad \text{Where N is the total number of components}$$

Summary of Parts Count Analysis

Parts count analysis is a simple analysis method that sums the failure rates of individual components within a system to estimate the system's failure frequency/likelihood.

Brief Summary of Characteristics

- Systematic, structured assessment relying on simple summation of component data to generate meaningful estimates of system failure frequencies/likelihoods

- Primarily performed by an individual analyst working with available component data and generic component failure data sources

- Quality of the evaluation depends on the quality of the system documentation, the quality of component data, and the training of the analyst

Most Common Uses

Parts count analysis is generally applicable for almost every type of analysis application, but is most effectively used for systems whose risk characteristics are dominated by single event failures.

It is often used as a rough screening approach for estimating reliability characteristics of systems, but can be effectively used to develop system failure rate predictions in relatively simple electronic and/or mechanical systems in which the system fails if any one part of the system fails.

Example Results

Example from the Reliability Analysis Center's *Reliability Toolkit*

Unit	Qty	Failure Rate (FPMH)*	Data Source	Data Source Environment	Environment Adjustment Factor	Total Failure Rate (FPMH)*
3.5" Disk Drives	2	40	Field	Office	1	80
CD-Rom Drive	3	10	Handbook	Office	1	30
Hard Drive	1	35	Vendor Test	Office	1	35
CPU Board	1	4	Field	Aircraft	.25	1
Keyboard	1	10	Field	Office	1	10
Monitor	1	40	Field	Aircraft	.25	10
Modem	1	3	Handbook	Office	1	3
Totals (FPMH)						169
MTBF (Hours)						5,917

*FPMH — Failures per million hours

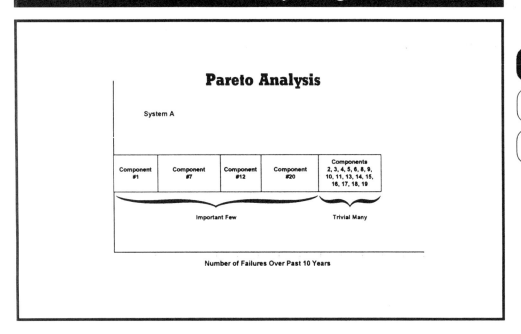

Pareto Analysis

System A

Number of Failures Over Past 10 Years

Screening Analysis

Broadly Applicable Detailed Analysis

Narrowly Focused Detailed Analysis

Summary of Pareto Analysis

Pareto analysis is a prioritization technique that identifies the most significant items among many. Employs the "80-20" rule, which states that 20% of the causes produce 80% of the effects.

Brief Summary of Characteristics

- Used as both a system-level and component-level analysis technique
- Yields broad quantitative results that are graphically depicted on simple bar charts
- Depending on the information analyzed, the technique generally requires some form of data tracking (e.g., monitoring the number or downtime hours caused by various events)
- Applicable to any operating system

Most Common Uses

Pareto analysis is most often used to rank system failure causes. Can be used to rank the causes that contribute to individual component failures. Also used to evaluate the reliability improvement resulting from system modifications with before and after data.

Example Results

Screening Analysis

Broadly Applicable Detailed Analysis

Narrowly Focused Detailed Analysis

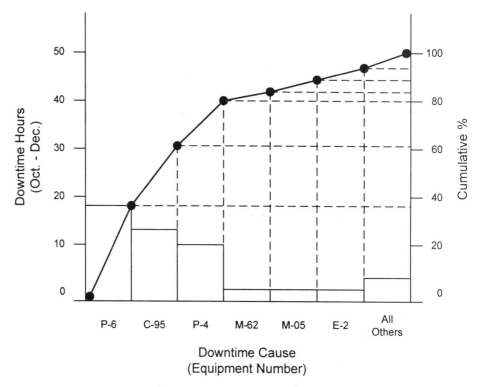

Pareto Graph of Downtime Contributors by Component

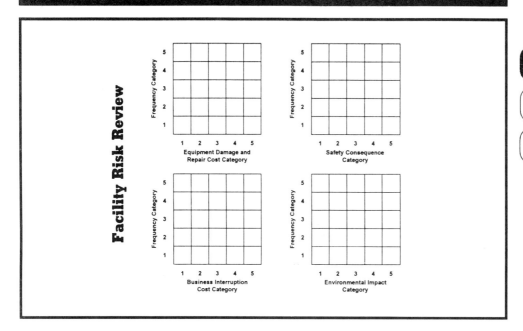

Screening Analysis

Broadly Applicable
Detailed Analysis

Narrowly Focused
Detailed Analysis

Summary of Facility Risk Review (FRR)

FRR uses systematic analyses at a high level to provide a broad characterization of potential problems and to (1) generate recommendations for improvements and (2) focus further, more detailed analysis on the most important areas.

Brief Summary of Characteristics

- Systematic process built on the same structure as used for more detailed failure modes and effects analyses or event tree analyses, but applied only at system/subsystem levels (not down to the component level)
- Generally applied to entire facilities
- Applicable to virtually any system, but typically used for manufacturing processes
- Generates:
  1) qualitative descriptions of scenarios leading to potential problems
  2) rough estimates of equipment damage, repair cost, business interruption cost, safety risks, environmental risks, etc.
  3) recommendations for improvements and/or more detailed analysis

Most Common Uses

FRR is primarily used to provide an effective screening of risks for entire facilities.

Example Results

Example Accident Frequency Categories

Category	Average Time Between Occurrences (Years)	Frequency (per Year)	Description
1	>300	<.003	Not expected to occur
2	100 – 300	.003 – .01	Not likely to occur during the lifetime of the plant
3	30 – 100	.01 – .03	Expected to occur no more than once during the lifetime of the plant
4	10 – 30	.03 – .1	Expected to occur no more than once or twice during the lifetime of the plant
5	3 – 10	.1 – .3	Expected to occur several times during the lifetime of the plant
6	1 – 3	.3 – 1.0	Expected to occur between once a year and once every three years
7	0.1-1	1.0-10.0	Expected to occur between once and ten times a year
8	0.01-0.1	10.0-100.0	Expected to occur between ten and one hundred times a year

Example Cost Categories

Category	Cost (1,000s of $)
1	Less than 1
2	1 - 10
3	10 - 50
4	50 - 250
5	250 - 1,000
6	1,000 - 5,000
7	More than 5,000

EQE International, Inc.

Example Results

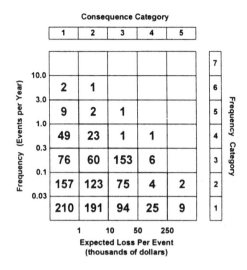

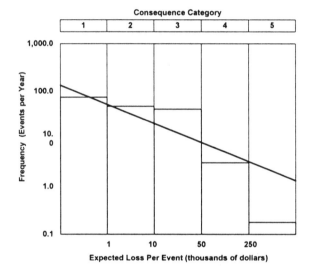

Screening Analysis

Broadly Applicable Detailed Analysis

Narrowly Focused Detailed Analysis

Relative Ranking

$$\text{Reliable Performance} \propto \text{Reliability Index} = \text{Fn}\left(\text{Factor}_1, \text{Factor}_2, \ldots\right)$$

Some example reliability index factors:

- ◆ robust design margins
- ◆ levels of redundancy
- ◆ human factors considerations
- ◆ vulnerability to external events
- ◆ use of proven technology
- ◆ etc.

Summary of Relative Ranking

Relative ranking uses attributes of a process or activity to calculate index numbers that are useful for making relative comparisons of various processes and activities (and in some cases can be correlated to actual performance estimates).

Brief Summary of Characteristics

- Very systematic process built on the experience of the ranking system developers
- Generally performed by an individual (sometimes a small group) trained to understand the ranking system, not necessarily reliability experts
- Based mostly on interviews, documentation reviews, and field inspections
- Used most often as a system-level analysis technique
- Applicable to almost any system or activity
- Generates:
  1) index numbers that provide ordered lists of processes or activities
  2) lists of attributes contributing most to lower rankings
- Quality of evaluation primarily determined by the relevance/quality of the ranking system and the training of the user(s)

Most Common Uses

Relative Ranking is primarily used to compare various situations/options.

It can be used to prioritize processes or activities for further evaluation according to their rankings.

Example Results

	Factor Scores						
	Design Margin	Level of Redundancy	Human Factors	Vulnerability to External Event	Proven Technology	• • •	
Option 1	9	3	7	5	8		64
Option 2	7	6	6	5	5		58
Option 3	5	9	7	5	3		55

Screening Analysis

Broadly Applicable Detailed Analysis

Narrowly Focused Detailed Analysis

Screening Analysis

Broadly Applicable Detailed Analysis

Narrowly Focused Detailed Analysis

Checklist Analysis/Human Factors Checklist Analysis

Evaluation Points	Yes	No	Not Evaluated	Comments
Subject Area 1				
Evaluation Point 1-1	✓			
Evaluation Point 1-2	✓			
Evaluation Point 1-3		✓		Recommendation A
•				
•				
Subject Area 2				
Evaluation Point 2-1			✓	
Evaluation Point 2-2	✓			
Evaluation Point 2-3	✓			
•				
•				
Subject Area 3				
•				
•				

Summary of Checklist Analysis

Checklist analysis is a systematic evaluation against pre-established criteria in the form of one or more checklists. General checklist analysis typically focuses on equipment issues with some human factors issues considered. A human factors checklist analysis uses a checklist that specifically addresses human factors issues.

Brief Summary of Characteristics

- Very systematic approach built on the historical knowledge included in checklist questions
- Used for system-level or component-level analysis
- Applicable to any system or procedure
- Generally performed by an individual (sometimes a small group) trained to understand the checklist questions, not necessarily reliability experts
- Based mostly on interviews, documentation reviews, and field inspections, and walk-throughs of the process
- Generates qualitative lists of conformance and nonconformance determinations with recommendations for correcting nonconformances
- Quality of evaluation primarily determined by the experience of people creating the checklist(s) and the training of the checklist user(s)

Most Common Uses

Checklist analysis most often used as a supplement or integral part of another method (especially what-if analysis) to address specific requirements, but seldom used alone because of the possibility of overlooking unique circumstances/issues not covered in the checklist.

Example Results

Example 1 — General Operability Checklist

B.   Piping and Valves

1. Is the piping specification suitable for the process conditions, considering:
   - compatibility with process materials and contaminants (e.g., corrosion and erosion resistance)?
   - compatibility with cleaning materials and methods (e.g., etching, steaming, pigging)?
   - normal pressure and temperature?
   - excess pressure (e.g., thermal expansion or vaporization of trapped liquids, blocked pump discharge, pressure regulator failure)?
   - high temperature (e.g., upstream cooler bypassed)?
   - low temperature (e.g., winter weather, cryogenic service)?
   - cyclical conditions (e.g., vibration, temperature, pressure)?
   - external corrosion because of the piping's design (e.g., material of construction, insulation on cold piping), location (e.g., submerged in a sump), or environment (e.g., saltwater spray)?

2. Is there any special consideration, for either normal or abnormal conditions, that could promote piping failure? For example:
   - Would flashing liquids autorefrigerate the piping below its design temperature?
   - Could accumulated water freeze in low points or in dead-end or intermittent service lines?
   - Could cryogenic liquid carry-over chill the piping below its design temperature?
   - Could heat tracing promote an exothermic reaction in the piping, cause solids to build up in the piping, or promote localized corrosion in the piping?
   - Could the pipe lining be collapsed by vacuum conditions?
   - Could a process upset cause corrosive material carry-over in the piping, or could dense corrosive materials (e.g., sulfuric acid) accumulate in valve seats, drain nipples, etc.?
   - In high temperature reducing service (e.g., hydrogen, methane, or carbon monoxide), could metal dusting cause catastrophic failure? Is the piping protected by suitable chemical addition (e.g., sulfides)?
   - Is the piping vulnerable to stress corrosion cracking (e.g., caustic in carbon steel piping, chlorides in stainless steel piping)? Should the piping be stress relieved?
   - Is the piping vulnerable to erosion? Are piping elbows and tees designed to minimize metal loss, and are they periodically inspected?
   - Could rapid valve closure or two-phase flow cause hydraulic hammer in the piping? Should valve opening/closing rates be dampened to avoid piping damage?
   - Are there flexible connections that could distort or crack?

3. Can piping sizes or lengths be reduced to minimize hazardous material inventories?

4. Have relief devices been installed in piping runs where thermal expansion of trapped fluids (e.g., chlorine) would separate flanges or damage gaskets?

5. Are piping systems provided with freeze protection, particularly cold water lines, instrument connections, and lines in dead-end service such as piping at standby pumps? Can the piping system be completely drained?

6. Were piping systems analyzed for stresses and movements resulting from thermal expansion and vibration? Are piping systems adequately supported and guided? Will any cast-iron valves be subjected to excessive stresses that could fracture them? Will pipe linings crack (particularly at the flange face) because of differential thermal expansion?

7. Are bellows, hoses, and other flexible piping connections really necessary? Could the piping system be redesigned to eliminate them? Are the necessary flexible connections strong enough for the service conditions?

8. What are the provisions for trapping and draining steam piping?

9. Which lines can plug? What are the hazards of plugged lines?

10. Are provisions made for flushing out all piping during startup and shutdown? Are hoses, spools, jumpers, etc., flushed or purged before use?

11. Are the contents of all lines identified?

12. Are there manifolds on any venting or draining systems and, if so, are there any hazards associated with the manifolds?

13. Are all process piping connections to utility systems adequately protected against potentially hazardous flows?
    - Are there check valves or other devices preventing backflow into the utility supply?
    - Are there disconnects (spools, hoses, swing elbows, etc.) with suitable blinds or plugs for temporary or infrequently used utility connections?
    - Are there double blocks and bleeds for permanent utility connections?

14. Are spray guards installed on pipe flanges in areas in which a spraying leak could injure operators or start fires?

15. Will the piping insulation trap leaking material and/or react exothermically with it?

16. Have plastic or plastic-lined piping systems been adequately grounded to avoid static buildup?

17. Are there remote shutoff devices on off-site pipelines that feed into the unit or storage tanks?

18. Can bypass valves (for control valves or other components) be quickly opened by operators?
    - What hazards may result if the bypass is opened (e.g., reverse flow, high or low level)?
    - What bypass valves are routinely opened to increase flow, and will properly sized control valves be installed?
    - Is the bypass piping arranged so it will not collect water and debris?
    - Is there a current log of open bypass valves kept in the control room so operators can ensure that they are reclosed if necessary in an emergency?

19. How are the positions of critical valves (block valves beneath relief devices, equipment isolation valves, dike drain valves, etc.) controlled (car seals, locks, periodic checks, etc.)?

20. How are the positions of critical valves (e.g., emergency isolation valves, dump valves) indicated to operators? Is the position of all nonrising stem valves readily apparent to the operators? Do control room displays directly indicate the valve position, or do they really indicate some other parameter, such as actuator position or torque, application of power to the actuator, or initiation of a control signal to the actuator?

21. . . . .

22. . . . .

23. . . . .

Etc.

Example 2 — Maintainability Checklist

A checklist is a basic technique used by maintainability personnel. It is simply a list of specific questions that provide a basis for determining whether good maintainability practices have been incorporated in the product design. The following are some of the common questions pertaining to many types of equipment. Each basic type of equipment should have its own checklist.

I. Accessibility
a. Are access doors or openings provided where periodic maintenance is expected?
b. Are the access doors quick-opening?
c. Are transparent windows available where observations are required to determine the need for maintenance?
d. Are access doors large enough to allow passage of replacement items?

II. Adjustments
a. Have adjustment frequencies been established?
b. Can adjustments be made without breaking seals?
c. Are adjustment areas easily accessible?
d. Are adjustment instructions readily available?
e. Can adjustments be made at the equipment site?
f. Are automatic stops used to prevent overriding the limit of adjustment?

III. Equipment
a. Are controls adequately labeled?
b. Are fuses mounted in the front of the equipment and can they be removed without use of special tools?
c. Are those components that are expected to need replacement readily available at the equipment?
d. Are components grouped functionally?
e. Are parts and components adequately labeled?

IV. Fasteners
a. Can standard tools be used on fasteners instead of special tools?
b. Are captive fasteners used where there is a possibility of lost fasteners causing excessive maintenance time?
c. Are standard fasteners used wherever possible?
d. Where fasteners require specific torque requirements, are instructions readily available?
e. . . .
f. . . .
g. . . .
Etc.

Example 3 — Condensed Human Factors Engineering Checklist

Static review of situation

1. Review of the equipment and procedure for obvious human factors violations
   a. Poor layout of controls and displays
   b. Inadequate labeling
   c. Legibility of labeling/markings
   d. Violation of populational stereotypes

2. Is the overall layout of the equipment/area consistent with average human dimensions and capabilities?
   a. Does equipment design support the initiation of the task (readily accessible and positioned logically with the rest of the system)?

3. Review the overall work environment
   a. Is the lighting adequate?
   b. Is the background noise level excessive?
   c. Are audible alarms detectible and not masked by other alarms?
   d. Is the temperature or ventilation excessively high or low?
   e. Are there established communication pathways with the rest of the system (verbal, headsets, phones, visual signals)
   f. Is the housekeeping in the area deficient?
   g. Is powered vehicle traffic nearby heavy?
   h. Are overhead cranes in the vicinity?
   i. Are there chemical exposure hazards nearby?
   j. Are there electrical shock hazards nearby?
   k. Are there high pressure hazards nearby?

4. Do procedures exist for the task?
   a. Is the procedure written?
   b. Is the procedure available when performing the task?
   c. Are equipment labels consistent with the procedure?
   d. Are personnel trained on the procedure?
   e. Is there periodic review/update of the procedure?

Dynamic review of situation

1. Are there initiation cues for the task or step?
   a. Does equipment design support the initiation of the task?
   b. Is there a procedure that initiates the task?
   c. Have the operators been trained on the meaning of the initiating cue?

2. Are the cues unambiguous and distinctive from the other signals?
   a. Are the controls and displays consistent with human factors design standards?
   b. Are the controls and displays consistent with the populational stereotypes of the group using the system?

3. Is the desired action clear?

4. Can the operator determine the current status of the system?

5. How difficult is it to compare the desired action to the current status of the system?

6. Can the operator correct the situation or perform the action within the required time period?

7. Is the feedback on control action prompt and direct?

Summary of What-if Analysis

Questions	Responses
■ "What if {a specific component} fails?" ■ "What if {a specific process upset} occurs?" ■ "What if {a specific human error} occurs?" ■ "What if {a specific external event} occurs?"	"That could result in {immediate system condition}" "That could potentially leading to {consequence of interest}" "That could only happen if {applicable safeguards} fail"

Screening Analysis

Broadly Applicable Detailed Analysis

Narrowly Focused Detailed Analysis

Summary of What-if Analysis

What-if analysis is a brainstorming approach that uses broad, loosely structured questioning to (1) postulate potential system upsets that may result in system performance problems, and (2) ensure that appropriate safeguards against those problems are in place.

Brief Summary of Characteristics

- Systematic, but loosely structured, assessment relying on brainstorming to generate a comprehensive review and a team of system experts to ensure that appropriate safeguards against system performance problems are in place
- Typically performed by one or more teams with diverse backgrounds and experience who participate in group review meetings of system documentation and field inspections
- Applicable to any system or procedure
- Used as a system-level or component-level analysis technique
- Generates qualitative descriptions of potential performance problems (in the form of questions and responses) as well as lists of recommendations for preventing problems
- Quality of the evaluation depends on the quality of the system documentation, the training of the review team leader, and the experience of the review team(s)

Most Common Uses

What-if analysis is generally applicable for almost every type of analysis application, especially those dominated by relatively simple failure scenarios.

What-if analysis is occasionally used alone, but most often used to supplement other, more structured techniques (especially checklist analysis).

Example Results

Summary of What-if Review of the Plant's Compressed Air System				
What if … ?	**Immediate System Condition**	**Ultimate Consequence**	**Safeguards**	**Actions**
1. The intake air filter begins to plug	Reduced air flow through the compressor affecting its performance	Inefficient compressor operation, leading to excessive energy usage and possible compressor damage Low/no air flow to production equipment and tools, leading to production inefficiencies and possibly outages	Pressure/vacuum gauge between the compressor and the intake filter Annual replacement of the filter Rain cap and screen at the air intake	Make a check of the pressure gauge reading part of a weekly round for someone OR Replace the local gauge with a low pressure switch that alarms in a manned area
2. Someone leaves a drain valve open	High air flow rate through the open valve to atmosphere	Low/no air flow to production equipment and tools, leading to production inefficiencies and possibly outages Potential for personnel injury from escaping air and/or blown debris	Small drain line would divert only a portion of the air flow, but maintaining pressure would be difficult	Require all drain lines to be capped when not in use
• • •	• • •	• • •	• • •	• • •

EQE International, Inc.

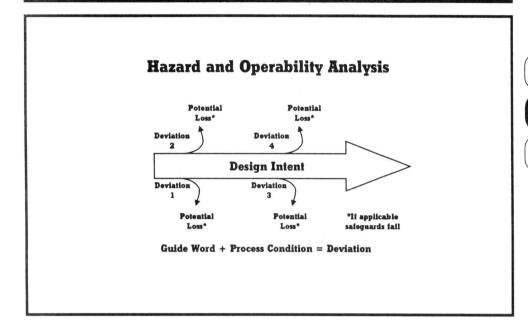

Hazard and Operability Analysis

Guide Word + Process Condition = Deviation

Screening Analysis

Broadly Applicable Detailed Analysis

Narrowly Focused Detailed Analysis

Summary of Hazard and Operability (HAZOP) Analysis

HAZOP is an inductive approach that uses a very systematic process (using special guide words) for postulating deviations from design intents for sections of systems and ensuring that appropriate safeguards are in place to help prevent system performance problems.

Brief Summary of Characteristics

- Systematic, highly structured assessment relying on HAZOP guidewords and team brainstorming to generate a comprehensive review and to ensure that appropriate safeguards against system performance problems are in place
- Typically performed by a multidisciplinary team
- Applicable to any system or procedure
- Used most as a system-level analysis technique
- Generates primarily qualitative results, although some basic quantification is possible

Most Common Uses

HAZOP is primarily used for identifying safety hazards and operability problems of continuous process systems (especially fluid and thermal systems). Can also be used to review procedures and sequential operations.

HAZOP Deviation Guide

Process Variables \ Guide Words	No, Not, None	Less, Low, Short	More, High, Long	Part Of	As Well As, Also	Other Than	Reverse
Flow	No Flow	Low Rate, Low Total	High Rate, High Total	Missing Ingredient	Misdirection, Impurities	Wrong Material	Backflow
Pressure	Open To Atmosphere	Low Pressure	High Pressure	—	—	—	Vacuum
Temperature	Freezing	Low Temperature	High Temperature	—	—	—	Auto-refrigeration
Level	Empty	Low Level	High Level	Low Interface	High Interface	—	—
Agitation	No Mixing	Poor Mixing	Excessive Mixing	Mixing Interruption	Foaming	—	Phase Separation
Reaction	No Reaction	Slow Reaction	Runaway Reaction	Partial Reaction	Side Reaction	Wrong Reaction	Decomposition
Time, Procedure	Skipped or Missing Step	Too Short, Too Little	Too Long, Too Much	Action(s) Skipped	Extra Action(s) (Shortcuts)	Wrong Action	Out of Order, Opposite
Speed	Stopped	Too Slow	Too Fast	Out of Sync	—	Web or Belt Break	Backward
Special	Utility Failure	External Leak	External Rupture	Tube Leak	Tube Rupture	Startup, Shutdown, Maintenance	—

Other Variables: Load, Concentration, Viscosity, pH, Static, Voltage, Current, etc.

Example Results — Equipment Analysis

Hazard and Operability Analysis of the Plant's Compressed Air System

Item	Deviation	Causes	Consequences	Safeguards	Recommendations
			1. Intake Line for the Compressor		
1.1	High flow		No consequences of interest		
1.2	Low/no flow	Plugging of filter or piping (especially at air intake) Rainwater accumulation in line	Inefficient compressor operation, leading to excessive energy usage and possible compressor damage Low/no air flow to production equipment and tools, leading to production inefficiencies and possibly outages	Pressure/vacuum gauge between the compressor and the intake filter Annual replacement of the filter Rain cap and screen at the air intake	Make a check of the pressure gauge reading part of a weekly round for someone OR Replace the local gauge with a low pressure switch that alarms in a manned area
1.3	Misdirected flow	No credible cause	• • •	• • •	• • •
• • •	• • •	• • •			

Example Results — Procedure Analysis

Hazard and Operability Analysis of the Procedure for Draining the Receiver in the Plant's Compressed Air

Item	Deviation	Causes	Consequences	Safeguards	Recommendations
			Step 4. Close the drain valve		
4.1	Skip	Technician distracted by other problems (especially if draining the liquid takes very long)	Low/no air flow to production equipment and tools, leading to production inefficiencies and possibly outages Potential for personnel injury from escaping air and/or blown debris	Small drain line would divert only a portion of the air flow, but maintaining pressure would be difficult	Require all drain lines to be capped when not in use
4.2	Too little	Valve sticks and operator incorrectly believes the valve is closed	Same effect as skipping the step, but to a lesser effect		
4.3	Too much	Not credible			
	• • •	• • •	• • •	• • •	• • •

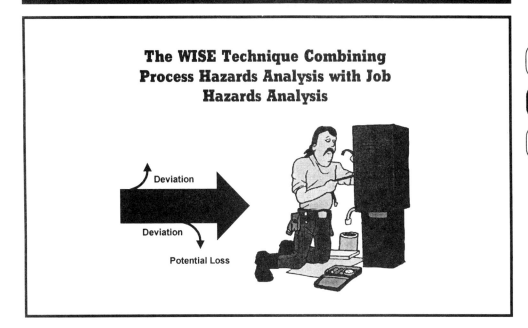

The WISE Technique Combining Process Hazards Analysis with Job Hazards Analysis

Screening Analysis

Broadly Applicable Detailed Analysis

Narrowly Focused Detailed Analysis

Summary of the Worker and Instruction Safety Evaluation (WISE) Technique

The worker and instruction safety evaluation technique is an efficient tool that integrates the hazard and operability (HAZOP) methodology that is often used for process hazards analysis (PHA) with job hazard analysis (JHA).

Brief summary of characteristics

- Systematic, highly structured assessment relying on WISEguides words (similar to HAZOP guide words) and brainstorming to generate a comprehensive review and ensure that appropriate safeguards against system performance problems and worker injury are in place
- Saves time when compared to doing separate job safety analysis and process hazards analysis
- Typically performed by a multidisciplinary team
- Applicable to any system or procedure
- Used most as a system-level analysis technique
- Generates primarily qualitative results, although some basic quantification is possible

Most common uses

WISE is primarily used for identifying safety hazards and operability of continuous process systems (especially fluid and thermal systems). Can also be used to review procedures and sequential operations.

WISEguides	Meaning
Skip/part of	The worker skips this step (or some part of it) and performs the rest of the procedure correctly. Example: The worker skipped Step X (open lube oil valve), so the compressor burned up when it was started in Step Y
More	The worker does too much of the specified action or does it too quickly. Example: The worker opened the valve too quickly, causing a water hammer which ruptured the steam line
Less	The worker does too little of the specified action or does it too slowly. Example: The worker added too little catalyst (Step X), so pressure built up when feed was added in Step Y, overpressurizing the reactor with unreacted feed material
Out of sequence	The worker performs the steps in a different order than specified by the procedure, possibly as a short cut. Example: The worker added both reactants before starting the mixer
Other than/reverse	The worker performs some action other than the one specified in the procedure, usually because of confusion or haste. Examples: When reaching for the Valve X control switch, the operator grasped and actuated the adjacent switch for Valve Y. After reinstalling the motor, the electrician wired it to run in reverse
Caught/in/on/by/between	The equipment entangles a body part or clothing, often because the machine guards are missing or inadequate. Example: The worker's arm was broken when it was caught on the spinning coupling
Struck by/contact by	The equipment or process material hits the worker. Examples: A forklift ran into a worker or a box toppled off a forklift onto a worker. Acid splashed out of a vat into a worker's eyes
Contact with/struck against	The worker inadvertently touches or hits the process. Examples: The pipefitter hit an unprotected light bulb and was electrocuted. The worker hit his head on a low pipe
Slip/trip/fall	The worker loses his/her grip or footing. Example: The worker dropped a wrench which punctured the top of the fiberglass tank

WISEguides	**Meaning**
Stress/strain/fatigue	The worker is poorly positioned with respect to the equipment, must frequently repeat a motion, or is overloaded. Example: The worker must carry 50-pound bags up a ladder and empty them into a tank
Exposure to	The process or location creates an acutely or chronically dangerous work environment — fumes, vibration, noise, heat, radiation, etc. Example: The worker may be exposed to fumes when taking a sample
Process upset/ malfunction	The process experiences an abnormal condition during this step of the procedure. Examples: The relief valve on Tank X discharges while the worker is checking the level on adjacent Tank Y. The belt breaks while the machine is being threaded
Layout/traffic/siting	The worker cannot approach or evacuate the area because of permanent or temporary obstructions. Example: The operator was run over as she sprinted from the control room to close an emergency isolation valve
Tools/equipment	The worker cannot perform the required actions because the necessary tools and equipment (including PPE) are not available. Example: The workers could not promptly isolate the release because the PPE cabinets were engulfed in the cloud

Example Results

Job Step	WISE-guides	Potential Consequences	Protection	Suggested Improvements
1	Skip	Debris in eye (Step 4)	Safety glasses	
		Asphyxiation (Step 4)	Room ventilation	
		Cylinder movement (Step 4)	Cylinder chained to rack	
			Cracking open connection (Step 3)	
	Less	See Skip		
	Contact with	Burned by steam	Insulated piping	
2	Skip	Debris in eye (Step 4)	Safety glasses	Wear respiratory protection when breaking connection.
		Toxic exposure (Step 3)	Room ventilation	
		Flammable release with possible fire (Step 4)	Cylinder chained to rack	Install check valve at catalyst pot
		Struck by pigtail (Step 4)	Cracking open connection (Step 3)	
	Less	See Skip		
	Contact with	Burned by steam	Insulated piping	
3	More	Debris in eye	Safety glasses	
	Out of Sequence	See Skip - Step 1 or 2		
	Caught between	Hand pinched between wrench and cylinder	Gloves	
	Slip	Wrench dropped	Safety shoes	Tether a wrench near the cylinder so it cannot hit the worker's foot
	Exposure to	Catalyst backflow (See Skip - Step 2)		
	Tools	Adjustable wrench slips off nut		Tether a correct-size wrench near the cylinder

Example Results (cont.)

Job Step	WISE-guides	Potential Consequences	Protection	Suggested Improvements
4	Caught between	Hand pinched between wrench and cylinder	Gloves	
	Struck by	Debris from connection or line	Safety glasses	Install check valve at catalyst pot
		Pigtail whipping	Cracking open connection (Step 3)	
		Cylinder falling over	Cylinder chained to rack	
	Slip	Wrench dropped	Safety shoes	Tether a wrench near the cylinder so it cannot hit the worker's foot
	Exposure to	Asphyxiation (See Skip - Step 1)		
		Catalyst backflow (See Skip - Step 2)		
	Tools	Adjustable wrench slips off nut		
				Tether a correct-size wrench near the cylinder

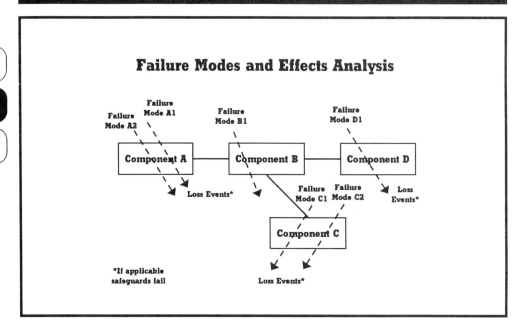

Summary of Failure Modes and Effects Analysis (FMEA)

FMEA is an inductive approach that (1) considers how the failure modes of each system component could result in system performance problems and (2) ensures that appropriate safeguards against such problems are in place. A quantitative version of FMEA is known as Failure Modes, Effects, and Criticality Analysis (FMECA).

Brief Summary of Characteristics

- Systematic, highly structured assessment relying on evaluation of component failure modes and team experience to generate a comprehensive review and ensure that appropriate safeguards against system performance problems are in place
- Used as a system-level and component-level analysis technique
- Applicable to any well-defined system
- Sometimes performed by an individual working with system experts through interviews and field inspections, but also can be performed by an interdisciplinary team with diverse backgrounds/experience participating in group review meetings of system documentation and field inspections
- Generates qualitative descriptions of potential performance problems (failure modes, root causes, effects, and safeguards) as well as lists of recommendations for reducing risks
- Can provide quantitative failure frequency and/or consequence estimates

Most Common Uses

FMEA is primarily used for reviews of mechanical and electrical systems.

Typical Failure Modes for Some Components

Component	Failure Mode
Pump	External leak External rupture Fails to start Fails off while running Starts prematurely Operates too long Operates at degraded head/flow performance (too fast, too slow, etc.)
Valves/Dampers	External leak External rupture Internal leak Plugged Fails to open Fails to close Fails to change position Spurious positioning Opens prematurely Closes prematurely
Gauges/Indicators/Recorders	Fails with no output signal Fails with a low output signal Fails with a high output signal Fails to respond to an input change Spurious output signal
Motor	Fails to start Fails off while running Starts prematurely Starts too late Operates too long Operates at degraded torque/rotational speed performance (runs backwards, too fast, too slow, etc.)

Example FMEA Table

Peripheral Equipment Subsystem for the Robot

	Failure Mode Event Identification		Failure Mode Cause and Effect Analysis		Failure Mode Frequency and Consequence Quantification							Failure Mode Evaluation	
Item	Component Description	Failure Mode	Failure Mode Causes	Failure Mode System Effects	Event Frequency (Event/YR)	Equipment Damage Cost ($/Event)	Business Interruption Cost ($/Event)	Repair Time Cost ($/Event)	Safety Category	Total Cost ($/Event)	Total Cost Risk ($/YR)	Failure Mode Safeguards and Commands	Recommended Actions for Failure Mode
1.1	Electric power source	Fails to supply power to motors	Internal circuit failures due to overheating, corrosion, vibrations, or impacts Defective fuse	Loss of drive power to all motion axes Potential damage to the end effector, equipment or parts in workspace, and damage to other equipment or injury to personnel in vicinity	4.836E-02	915.75	4,268.30	244.14	4	5,428.19	262.51	Insuring proper install./ maint., high initial quality, and isolation from the environment are key operating parameters. These should be addressed in install./maint. and design Loss of motion may allow other interacting equipment to damage the robot	Recs. 1 and 2 for install./maint. and design Rec. 15 for shutting down feed lines and interacting equipment during robot loss of power or error signal Rec. 16 for using an alternative power source to send loss of power signal Rec. 17 for requiring recalibration of robot, with manual initiation, after error or loss of power equipment
1.2	Electric power source	Fails to limit current to motors	Incorrect or defective fuse Incorrect current set for operation	Damage to motors or motor drivers with loss of single or multiple axis motion Potential damage to the end effector, equipment or parts in workspace, and damage or injury to other equipment or personnel in vicinity	1.472E-03	774.65	3,899.54	212.53	3	4,886.72	7.19	Insuring proper install./ maint., high initial quality, are key operating parameters. These should be addressed in install./ maint. and design	Recs. 1 and 2 for install./maint. and design

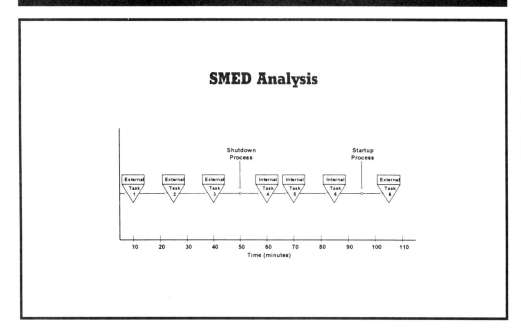

Screening Analysis

Broadly Applicable Detailed Analysis

Narrowly Focused Detailed Analysis

Summary of Single Minute Exchange of Dies (SMED) Analysis

Single minute exchange of dies is a manufacturing strategy that originated in Japan to help facilitate quick changeovers (for product types, etc.) and reduce system downtime. The SMED methodology has successfully been applied to maintenance activities to help reduce system downtime during various maintenance tasks (i.e., reducing MDT).

Brief summary of characteristics

- Systematic, structured approach applied to a maintenance activity that identifies the specific tasks, the task completion time, the tools and materials needed, and whether the task is external (done while process running) or internal (done while process down)
- Applicable for any maintenance task, but most beneficial for tasks that require system downtime
- Typically performed by a multidisciplinary team
- Generally requires a "live" situation time study

Most common uses

- Most often used to analyze common maintenance activities (scheduled and unscheduled) and switchovers of equipment from one product to another

General Guidelines for SMED Analysis

Screening Analysis

Broadly Applicable
Detailed Analysis

Narrowly Focused
Detailed Analysis

1. Perform Pareto analysis to determine the maintenance activities that result in the largest amount of downtime. (Determine if root causes are addressed before proceeding)

2. Assign team to observe the maintenance work activities with the largest downtime contribution. Analyze each task within the activity and document the time required for each specific task. Plot the results on a bar graph or enter into a table

3. Differentiate the tasks as external (done while system operating) or internal (done while system down)

4. Eliminate any unnecessary tasks, especially internal tasks

5. Convert as many internal tasks to external tasks as possible

6. Brainstorm ways to streamline the remaining internal and external tasks
   — think of ways to better organize people, tools, parts, materials
   — think of ways to ensure the activity is uninterrupted (e.g., schedule around shift changes, lunches, breaks)

7. Decide what ideas to adopt and test
   — determine feasibility of ideas
   — test and implement those that will contribute the most

8. Develop/update the maintenance procedure

9. Prepare and conduct the next maintenance activity using the updated procedure
   — perform steps 2 through 8 until the maintenance activity is optimized

10. Change procedure as new ideas develop to allow continuous improvement

Note: While striving to move internal tasks to external tasks (which are performed while equipment is running), be aware of possible safety issues

Example Results

SMED Analysis — Pump P-65				
	Prior to Analysis		Post Analysis	
Task	Time (mins)	External/ Internal	External/ Internal	Time (mins)
1. Obtain SAFETY WORK PERMIT/HF ACID AREA before entering unit	10	E	E	10
2. Find Field Operator to: • Discuss hazards of the task/additional PPE required • Obtain location/operational status of safety equipment • Gather information on/troubleshoot equipment problems	13	E	E	13
Shutdown				
3. Complete lockout/tagout (if required for task): a. Physically verify lockout-tagout b. Put lock/tag on box/equipment c. Record lockout-tagout information in Lockout/Tagout Log Book	8	I	I	8
4. Obtain confined space entry permit	15	I	E	15
5. Remove insulation from pump (as required)	3	I	E	3
6. Physically verify pump is depressurized	1	I	I	1
7 Install blinds and disassemble pump as needed to troubleshoot and remove defective parts	28	I	I	28
8. Obtain the correct replacement parts from warehouse	12	I	I	12
9. Repair/replace parts as needed (verify acceptable tolerances)	11	I	I	11
10. Reassemble pump and reinstall pump • Verify gaskets and sealing surfaces are in good condition • Verify acceptable tolerances	22	I	I	22
11. Document repair on pump data sheet	4	I	E	4
12. Remove blinds	7	I	I	7
13. Clean up work area and verify all guards are in place	4	I	E/I	2/2
14. Reverse lockout/tagout: a. Remove lock/tag from box/equipment b. Sign out of Lockout/Tagout Log Book	6	I	I	6
15. Notify field Operator and Maintenance Supervisor that task is complete	2	I	I	2
16. Reinstall insulation	4	I	E	4
Startup				
17. Verify repairs are satisfactory after startup: • Verify there are no leaks • Verify suction/discharge pressure • Verify vibration is not excessive	5	E	E	5
Total Time	155			155
Internal	127			99
External	28			56

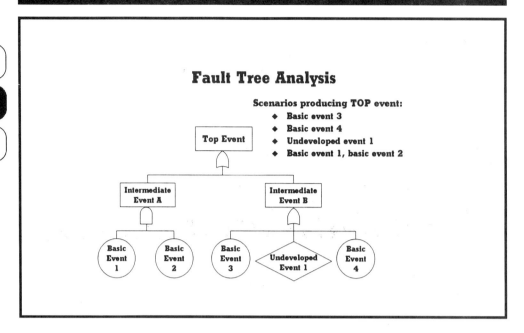

Screening Analysis

Broadly Applicable Detailed Analysis

Narrowly Focused Detailed Analysis

Fault Tree Analysis

Scenarios producing TOP event:
- Basic event 3
- Basic event 4
- Undeveloped event 1
- Basic event 1, basic event 2

Summary of Fault Tree Analysis (FTA)

Deductive analysis that graphically models (using Boolean logic) how logical relationships between equipment failures, human errors, and external events can combine to cause system performance problems.

Brief Summary of Characteristics

- Systematic, highly structured assessment relying on the analyst's experience to generate a comprehensive review and ensure that appropriate safeguards against system performance problems are in place

- Used most as a system-level analysis technique

- Consideration of human errors and common-cause failures strongly influences results

- Primarily performed by an individual working with system experts through interviews and field inspections

- Generates:
  1) qualitative descriptions of potential reliability problems (combinations of events causing specific reliability problems of interest)
  2) quantitative estimates of failure frequencies/likelihoods and relative importances of various failure sequences/contributing events
  3) lists of recommendations for reducing risks
  4) quantitative evaluations of recommendation effectiveness

- Quality of the evaluation depends on the quality of the system documentation, the training of the analyst, and the experience of the subject matter experts assisting the analyst

Most Common Uses

FTA is generally applicable for almost every type of analysis application, but most effectively used to address the fundamental causes of specific reliability problems dominated by relatively complex combinations of events.

Example Results

Example Fault Tree

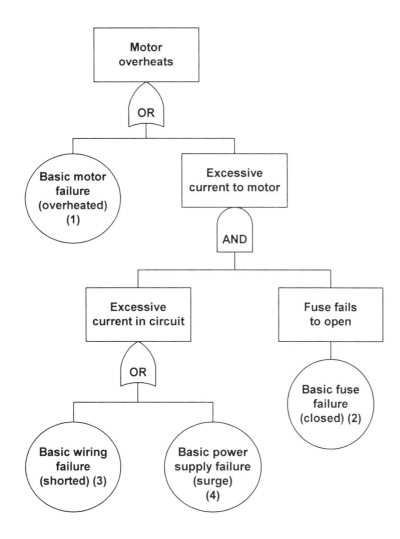

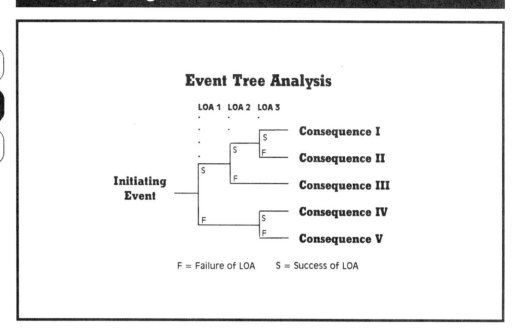

Screening Analysis

Broadly Applicable Detailed Analysis

Narrowly Focused Detailed Analysis

Event Tree Analysis

LOA 1 LOA 2 LOA 3

Initiating Event

S — Consequence I
F — Consequence II
F — Consequence III
S — Consequence IV
F — Consequence V

F = Failure of LOA   S = Success of LOA

Summary of Event Tree Analysis (ETA)

ETA is an inductive analysis that graphically models (using decision trees) the possible outcomes from an initiating event capable of producing a consequence of interest.

Brief Summary of Characteristics

- Systematic, highly structured assessment relying on the analyst's experience to generate a comprehensive review and ensure that appropriate safeguards against system performance problems are in place

- Primarily performed by an individual working with system experts through interviews and field inspections

- Generates:
  1) qualitative descriptions of potential reliability problems (combinations of events producing various types of problems from initiating events)
  2) quantitative estimates of event frequencies/likelihoods and relative importances of various failure sequences/contributing events
  3) lists of recommendations for reducing risks
  4) quantitative evaluations of recommendation effectiveness

- Quality of the evaluation depends on the quality of the system documentation, the training of the analyst, and the experience of the subject matter experts assisting the analyst

Most Common Uses

ETA is generally applicable for almost every type of analysis application, but most effectively used to address possible outcomes of initiating events for which multiple safeguards (lines of assurance) are in place as protective features.

Screening Analysis

Broadly Applicable Detailed Analysis

Narrowly Focused Detailed Analysis

Example Results

Initiating Event	Feed Shut Off	Blowdown Works	Accident Sequence Number	Frequency (Events/yr)	Consequence
High pressure in separator (1/yr)	0.9 Yes		LOC-1	0.9	4-hour loss of production
	No 0.1	0.94	LOC-2	0.094	2-day loss of production
		0.06	LOC-3	0.006	Severe damage, 3-month outage

Screening Analysis

Broadly Applicable Detailed Analysis

Narrowly Focused Detailed Analysis

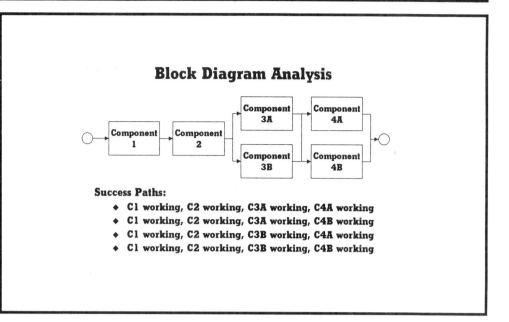

Block Diagram Analysis

Success Paths:
- C1 working, C2 working, C3A working, C4A working
- C1 working, C2 working, C3A working, C4B working
- C1 working, C2 working, C3B working, C4A working
- C1 working, C2 working, C3B working, C4B working

Summary of Block Diagram Analysis

Block diagram analysis is a deductive analysis that graphically models (using simple block diagrams) the combinations of system functions that provide successful system operations.

Brief Summary of Characteristics

- Systematic, highly structured assessment relying on the analyst's experience to generate a comprehensive review and ensure that appropriate safeguards against undesirable events are in place

- Primarily performed by an individual working with system experts through interviews and field inspections

- Generates:
  1) qualitative descriptions of system functions that must be preserved to avoid undesirable events
  2) quantitative estimates of reliability-related characteristics
  3) lists of recommendations for reducing risks
  4) quantitative evaluations of recommendation effectiveness

- Quality of the evaluation depends on the quality of the system documentation, the training of the analyst, and the experience of the subject matter experts assisting the analyst

Most Common Uses

Block diagram analysis is generally applicable for almost every type of analysis application, but most effectively used to model the key system functions for preventing undesirable events and to set reliability achievement goals for various sections of a system (especially useful for systems whose risk characteristics are dominated by relatively complex combinations of events).

Screening Analysis

Broadly Applicable Detailed Analysis

Narrowly Focused Detailed Analysis

Example Results

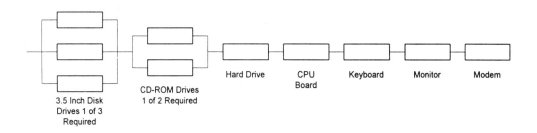

Hard Drive   CPU Board   Keyboard   Monitor   Modem

3.5 Inch Disk Drives 1 of 3 Required

CD-ROM Drives 1 of 2 Required

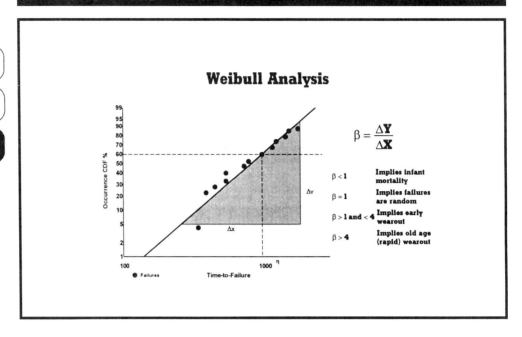

Summary of Weibull Analysis

Weibull analysis is a failure analysis and prediction technique that statistically models component failures, even with small samples of failure data.

Brief Summary of Characteristics

- Used most often as a component-level analysis technique
- Quality of the evaluation largely depends on the quality of the failure data that are used. Requires data tracking (e.g., monitoring the time to failure for a specific component)
- Yields quantitative results that are graphically depicted in a Weibull chart
- Parameters from the Weibull plot can be used to help determine the failure mechanism for the component being analyzed
- Primarily performed by an individual

Most Common Uses

Weibull analysis is primarily used for failure analysis of mechanical components for which good age-to-failure data are available.

Example Results

Weibull Analysis Process

A manufacturer estimates that its customers will operate a product (a pneumatically powered tool) for 4,000 hours per year, on average. The company wants to sell the log splitter with a 1-year warranty, but it needs to estimate the percentage of returns that will be experienced in order to assess the warranty cost. The manufacturer authorizes a test program using 10 random samples of the product to begin its analysis.

Ranked Times to Failure

Sample Number	Rank Order (i)	Time to Failure (hours)
6	1	5,005
3	2	6,000
10	3	7,000
8	4	8,500
2	5	9,750
4	6	10,075
7	7	13,025
5	8	15,000
9	9	15,050
1	10	18,200

X-Y Coordinates for Weibull Plots

Sample Number	Rank Order (i)	X-Coordinate Time to Failure (hours)	Y-Coordinate Median Rank (percent)
6	1	5,005	6.70
3	2	6,000	16.32
10	3	7,000	25.94
8	4	8,500	35.57
2	5	9,750	45.19
4	6	10,075	54.81
7	7	13,025	64.43
5	8	15,000	74.06
9	9	15,050	83.68
1	10	18,200	93.30

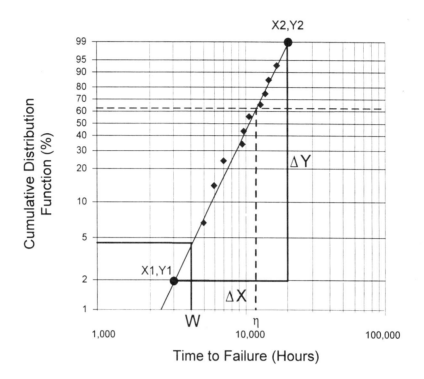

The characteristic life, η, is estimated from the graph at the intercept of the plotted line and the 63.2% CDF value by dropping a vertical line to the x-axis. For the example, the characteristic life of the tool indicates that after approximately 12,000 hours of operation (3 years), almost two-thirds of the tools will have "worn out."

In addressing the manufacturer's original question, approximately 4.5% of the tools (determined by the Y value corresponding to 4,000 hours on the time to failure axis) will have to be replaced with new tools in the 4,000-hour warranty period.

Example results

Facing a short-term budgetary crisis, a production manager decided to consider running a critical, continuously-operating, screw conveyor for an additional one year beyond its scheduled overhaul. Because the production manager was concerned about the financial risk associated with a catastrophic screw conveyor failure (expected to cost the company $25,000, including business interruption costs), the manager asked the maintenance engineer to assess the risk of delaying the overhaul and compare that risk to the expected cost of performing the overhaul now (expected to cost the company $15,000, including business interruption costs). If the **current value** of the deferred overhaul expense plus the financial risk of delaying the overhaul were less than the $15,000 required for the overhaul now, the manager would authorize the delay.

The maintenance engineer collected company-wide failure data (as well as some industry-specific data available from equipment vendors) for this type of screw conveyor. Next, the engineer analyzed the data and developed the failure rate curve shown below.

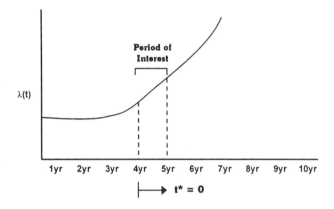

Failure rate over period of interest:

$$\lambda\left(\mathbf{t}^{*}\right) = \lambda\left(\mathbf{t} - \mathbf{4yr}\right)$$

Probability of failure during period of interest:

$$\overline{\mathbf{R}}\left(\mathbf{t}^{*} = \mathbf{0} \to \mathbf{t}^{*} = \mathbf{1yr}\right) = \mathbf{1} - \mathbf{e}^{-\int_{\mathbf{t}^{*}=\mathbf{0}}^{\mathbf{t}^{*}=\mathbf{1yr}} \lambda\left(\mathbf{t}^{*}\right)\mathbf{dt}^{*}}$$

From this function, the maintenance engineer estimated a 20% chance of the conveyor failing to survive to 5 years (1 year beyond the planned rebuild life of 4 years) without a catastrophic failure. Thus, the maintenance engineer advised the production manager that delaying the overhaul posed a 20% chance of experiencing a $25,000 expense within the next year and an 80% chance of experiencing a $15,000 expense within the next year. (The $15,000 expense next year is equivalent to a $13,600 expense this year in "today's dollars," based on the 10% discount rate). Thus, the maintenance engineer calculated that delaying the overhaul effectively "cost" the company $15,900 (i.e, 20% x $25,000 + 80% x $13,600) this year compared to the $15,000 cost of performing the overhaul now. Because of this insight, the production manager decided to go ahead with the overhaul and explore other ways of cutting near-term costs.

Screening Analysis

Broadly Applicable
Detailed Analysis

**Narrowly Focused
Detailed Analysis**

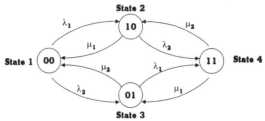

Markov Analysis

Two-component system:
- State 1: Both working, system working
- State 2: Component 1 failed,
  component 2 working, system working
- State 3: Component 1 working,
  component 2 failed, system working
- State 4: Both failed, system failed

Summary of Markov Analysis

Markov analysis is a model of all possible states of a system (and transitions between states) that allows an analyst to calculate frequencies/probabilities of system failure states.

Brief Summary of Characteristics

- Systematic, highly structured assessment relying on the analyst's experience to generate a comprehensive review and ensure that appropriate safeguards against undesirable events are in place

- Primarily performed by an individual analyst working with system experts through interviews and field inspections

- Generates:
  1) qualitative descriptions of potential failure states producing undesirable events (combinations of events causing specific problems of interest)
  2) quantitative estimates of event frequencies/likelihoods and relative importances of various failure sequences/contributing events
  3) lists of recommendations for reducing risks
  4) quantitative evaluations of recommendation effectiveness

- Quality of the evaluation depends on the quality of the system documentation, the training of the analyst, and the experience of the subject matter experts assisting the analyst

Most Common Uses

Markov analysis is generally applicable for almost every type of analysis application, but is most effectively used to address the fundamental causes of specific undesirable events dominated by relatively complex combinations of events.

It is only used when simpler analysis forms (such as fault tree analysis and block diagram modeling) cannot be used to model a situation appropriately.

Screening Analysis

Broadly Applicable Detailed Analysis

Narrowly Focused Detailed Analysis

Screening Analysis

Broadly Applicable
Detailed Analysis

Narrowly Focused
Detailed Analysis

Simulation Modeling

$$\begin{array}{l}\text{Overall System}\\ \text{Performance}\\ \text{Characteristic}\end{array} = Fn\left(Performance_{subsystem\,1}, \cdot \cdot \cdot, Performance_{subsystem\,N}\right)$$

Where

Performance$_{subsystem\,i}$ depends on many factors, including potential failures

Summary of Simulation Modeling

Simulation modeling incorporates reliability-related characteristics into overall process simulation models so that failure and repair issues can be appropriately accounted for in overall models of process performance (e.g., throughput).

Brief Summary of Characteristics

- Sophisticated mathematical modeling approaches implemented through commercially available system modeling software (sometimes with modifications/extensions to better handle failure and repair models)
- Generates more complete models of overall performance for systems as well as traditional reliability-related characteristics (reliability, availability, mean-time-between-failures, etc.)
- Identifies dominant contributors to potential performance problems

Most Common Uses

Simulation modeling can be incorporated into any process simulation, but is typically applied only for highly critical operations (space applications, nuclear applications, etc.).

Human Reliability Analysis

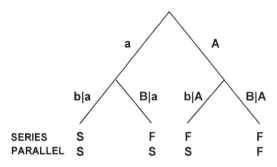

Screening Analysis

Broadly Applicable
Detailed Analysis

Narrowly Focused
Detailed Analysis

TASK "A" = THE FIRST TASK

TASK "B" = THE SECOND TASK

    a = PROBABILITY OF SUCCESSFUL PERFORMANCE OF TASK "A"

    A = PROBABILITY OF UNSUCCESSFUL PERFORMANCE OF TASK "A"

  b|a = PROBABILITY OF SUCCESSFUL PERFORMANCE OF TASK "B"
          GIVEN a

  B|a = PROBABILITY OF UNSUCCESSFUL PERFORMANCE OF TASK "B"
          GIVEN a

  b|A = PROBABILITY OF SUCCESSFUL PERFORMANCE OF TASK "B"
          GIVEN A

  B|A = PROBABILITY OF UNSUCCESSFUL PERFORMANCE OF TASK "B"
          GIVEN A

FOR THE SERIES SYSTEM:

    $\Pr[S] = a(b|a)$

    $\Pr[F] = 1 - a(b|a) = a(B|a) + A(b|A) + A(B|A)$

FOR THE PARALLEL SYSTEM:

    $\Pr[S] = 1 - A(B|A) = a(b|a) + a(B|a) + A(b|A)$

    $\Pr[F] = A(B|A)$

Summary of Human Reliability Analysis (HRA)

HRA is a specialized inductive graphical analysis tool (similar in form to fault tree analysis and event tree analysis) designed for evaluating human sequential operations. HRA accounts for various human errors and recovery actions as well as equipment failures.

Brief Summary of Characteristics

- Systematic, highly structured assessment relying on the analyst's experience to generate a comprehensive review and ensure that appropriate safeguards against undesirable events are in place

Screening Analysis

Broadly Applicable
Detailed Analysis

Narrowly Focused
Detailed Analysis

- Primarily performed by an individual working with system experts through interviews and field inspections
- Generates:
  1) qualitative descriptions of potential undesirable events (combinations of events producing various types of undesirable events as a result of human errors at various steps of a procedure)
  2) quantitative estimates of failure frequencies/likelihoods and relative importances of various accident sequences/contributing events
  3) lists of recommendations for reducing risks
  4) quantitative evaluations of recommendation effectiveness

- Quality of the evaluation depends on the quality of the system documentation, the training of the analyst, and the experience of the subject matter experts assisting the analyst

Most Common Uses

HRA is exclusively used for detailed evaluation of human operations (especially procedural tasks); it is most often used as a supplement to a broader analysis using another technique.

HRA is best suited for situations in which complex combinations of errors/ equipment failures are necessary for undesirable events to occur.

It is often used in conjunction with checklist analyses that focus on specific human reliability issues such as error-likely situations.

Example Results

HRA Example

Assume that the system described below exists in a process unit recently purchased by your company. As the manager, the safety of this unit is now your responsibility. You are concerned because your process hazard analysis team identified the potential for an operator error to result in a rupture of the propane condenser. You have chartered an HRA to estimate the likelihood of the condenser rupturing as the result of such an error and to identify ways to reduce the expected frequency of such ruptures.

System Description

Four parallel propane condensers, one of which is illustrated in the figure below, are designed with a 450-psig shell pressure rating and a 125-psig tube pressure rating. The propane vapor pressure is controlled at 400 psig; the cooling water flowing through the condenser tubes is normally maintained at 75 psig. Liquid propane flows out of the condenser as soon as it condenses; no significant inventory of liquid propane is left in the condenser. The two propane isolation valves for each condenser are rising-stem gate valves with no labels. The two water isolation valves for each condenser are butterfly valves with no labels. Their handwheel actuators have position indicators.

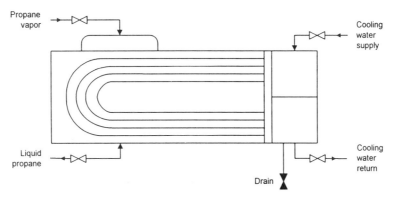

Propane Condenser Schematic

A tube has failed in one of the four condensers about once every three years. If a condenser tube fails, the affected condenser can be removed from service by closing four isolation valves (propane vapor inlet valve, liquid propane outlet valve, cooling water supply valve, and cooling water return valve). However, if a tube fails, it is essential that the operator close the two propane isolation valves before closing the two water isolation valves. Closing the two water valves first would allow pressure to build on the tube side of the condenser and rupture the tube head.

Analyzed System Conditions

- A tube has failed in the condenser
- The low depropanizer pressure alarm has sounded in the control room
- The experienced field operator has observed water and gas spewing from the hydrocarbon vent at the cooling tower. The field operator shouts over the radio that a propane vapor cloud appears to be forming and moving toward the control room
- The control room operator has directed the field operator to isolate the failed condenser as quickly as possible so that a unit shutdown will not be necessary
- The operator must close the valves by hand. If a valve sticks, there is no time to go get tools to help close the valve — the process must be shut down
- The field operator has correctly identified the condenser with the failed tube by the sound of the expanding propane and the visible condensation/frost on the shell

Events Included in the HRA Event Tree

Failure Symbol	Failure Description	Estimated Probability
A	Operator fails to close the propane valves first	0.05
Σ_1	Propane inlet valve sticks open	0.001
Σ_2	Propane outlet valve sticks open	0.001
B	Operator fails to detect a stuck valve	0.025
C	Operator chooses to close the cooling water valves to stop the propane release	0.25

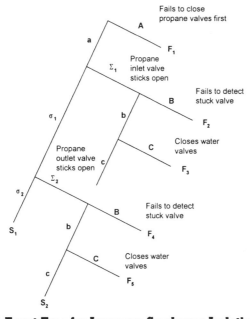

HRA Results

$F_1 = A$	$= 5.0 \times 10^{-2}$
$F_2 = a\Sigma_1 B$	$= 2.4 \times 10^{-5}$
$F_3 = a\Sigma_1 bC$	$= 2.3 \times 10^{-4}$
$F_4 = a\sigma_1\Sigma_2 B$	$= 2.4 \times 10^{-5}$
$F_5 = a\sigma_1\Sigma_2 bC$	$= 2.3 \times 10^{-4}$
$F_T = F_1 + \ldots + F_5$	$= 0.05$

HRA Event Tree for Improper Condenser Isolation

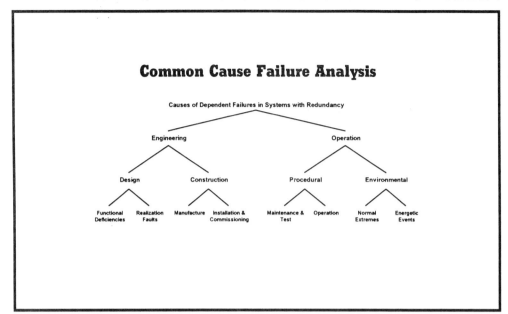

Common Cause Failure Analysis

Causes of Dependent Failures in Systems with Redundancy

Screening Analysis

Broadly Applicable Detailed Analysis

Narrowly Focused Detailed Analysis

Summary of Common Cause Failure Analysis (CCFA)

CCFA is a specialized approach for systematically examining sequences of events stemming from the conduct of operations and/or operation of physical systems that cause multiple failures/errors to occur from the same root causes, thus defeating multiple layers of protection simultaneously.

Brief Summary of Characteristics

- Systematic, structured assessment relying on the analyst's experience and guidelines for identifying potential dependencies among failure events to generate a comprehensive review and ensure that appropriate safeguards against common cause failure events are in place

- Used most as a system-level analysis technique

- Primarily performed by an individual working with system experts through interviews and field inspections

- Generates:
  1) qualitative descriptions of possible dependencies among events
  2) quantitative estimates of dependent failure frequencies/likelihoods
  3) lists of recommendations for reducing dependencies among failure events

- Quality of the evaluation depends on the quality of the system documentation, the training of the analyst, and the experience of the subject matter experts assisting the analyst

Most Common Uses

CCFA is exclusively used as a supplement to a broader analysis using another technique, especially fault tree and event tree analyses.

It is best suited for situations in which complex combinations of errors/equipment failures are necessary for undesirable events to occur.

Example Results

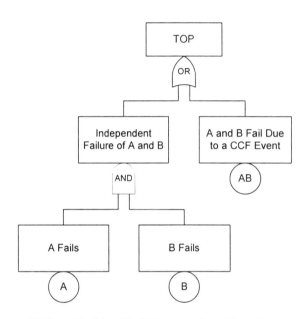

Failure Model with CCF Event Considerations

Guidelines on Redundancy and Diversity

System Type	Failure Probability Omitting CCF	Failure Probability Considering CCF
Mechanical, 1 Train	10^{-2}	10^{-2}
Mechanical, 2 Redundant Trains	10^{-4}	10^{-3}
Mechanical, 3 Redundant Trains	10^{-6}	5×10^{-4}
Mechanical, 2 Diverse, Redundant Trains	10^{-4}	2×10^{-4}
Electronic, 1 Train	10^{-4}	10^{-4}
Electronic, 2 Redundant Trains	10^{-8}	10^{-5}
Electronic, 3 Redundant Trains	10^{-12}	10^{-5}
Electronic, 2 Diverse, Redundant Trains	10^{-8}	10^{-6}

EQE International, Inc.

Software Failure Analysis

- **Traditional — techniques such as**
  - ◆ fault tree analysis
  - ◆ FMEA
  - ◆ review of procedures
- **Specialized — numerous models for predicting and estimating software reliability (typically based on data from fault detection activities)**

Screening Analysis

Broadly Applicable Detailed Analysis

Narrowly Focused Detailed Analysis

Summary of Software Failure Analysis

Software failure analysis is an assortment of tools for managing software development and predicting software reliability.

Brief Summary of Characteristics

- Structured guidelines and experience of analysts generate reviews of software products in varying levels of detail and ensure that appropriate safeguards against undesirable events are in place
- Primarily performed by an individual working with software experts through interviews and source code reviews
- Generates:
  1) qualitative descriptions of software weaknesses
  2) statistical estimates of failure frequencies/likelihoods for software modules
  3) lists of recommendations for reducing risks
- Quality of the evaluation depends on the quality of the software documentation, the training of the analyst, and the experience of the subject matter experts assisting the analyst

Most Common Uses

Software failure analysis is exclusively used to analyze potential failures in important (or "critical") software modules. It is most often used as a supplement to a broader analysis using another more general technique.

Software Reliability Prediction Models

- Rome Laboratory TR-92-52
- Rome Laboratory TR-92-15
- Musa's Execution Time Model
- Putnam's Model
- Historical Data Collection

Software Reliability Estimation Models

- Fault Count
  - Exponential
  - Shooman Model
  - Lloyd-Lipow Model
  - Musa's Basic Model
  - Musa's Logarithmic Model
  - Goel-Okumoto Model
- Historical Data Collection Model
- Raleigh Models
  - Schnick-Wolverton Model
- Weibull Models
- Test Coverage Models
  - IEEE Test Coverage Model
  - Leone's Test Coverage Model
  - Test Success Model
- Tagging Models
  - Seeding
  - Dual Test Group Model
- Bayesian Models
- Thompson and Chelson's Model

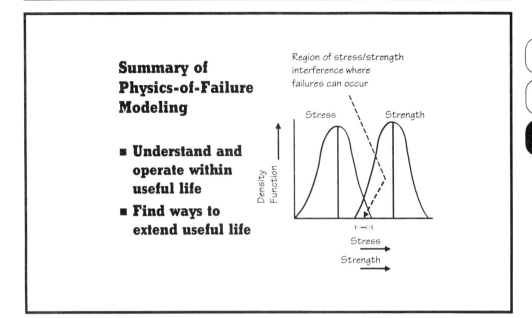

Summary of Physics-of-Failure Modeling

■ **Understand and operate within useful life**

■ **Find ways to extend useful life**

Region of stress/strength interference where failures can occur

Stress   Strength

Density Function

Stress

Strength

Screening Analysis

Broadly Applicable Detailed Analysis

Narrowly Focused Detailed Analysis

Summary of Physics-of-Failure Modeling

Physics-of-failure modeling defines relationships between key technical parameters associated with components (e.g., number of cycles, stress loads, exposures to energy sources, contact with various materials) and reliability-related characteristics (particularly time to failure).

Brief Summary of Characteristics

- Highly technical in nature
- Primarily useful to designers, but can be beneficial to groups monitoring equipment performance (operators, maintenance technicians, inspectors, etc.)
- Addresses a wide range of technical topic areas and disciplines (mechanics, electronics, structures, etc.)
- Provides insight into how to avoid failures, but does not directly produce recommendations
- Quality of models depends on technical understanding of the physics affecting failures

Most Common Uses

Physics-of-Failure Modeling is used in virtually all industries for establishing design guidelines and guidelines for monitoring/extending field use of equipment.

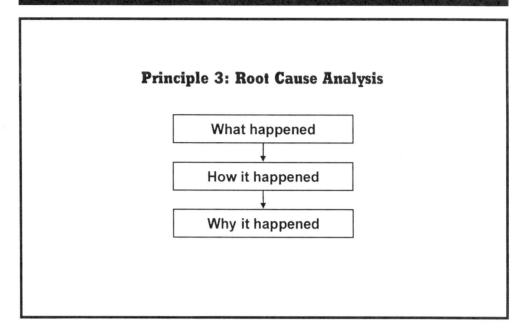

Principle 3: Root Cause Analysis

What happened

↓

How it happened

↓

Why it happened

If our activities associated with Principles 1 and 2 work perfectly, the activities associated with Principle 3 will not be needed. However, things do not always work as we expect and we need a method to prevent problems from recurring.

Root cause analysis requires us to look not only at what happened, but how it happened and why it happened. By understanding how and why the event happened we can develop more effective solutions.

The recommendations we develp from a root cause analysis feed back into Principles 1 and 2. The recommendations will require us to modify our management systems (Principle 1) or to perform proactive analysis (Principle 2). In this way, the three principles are related.

Idealized Process Operation

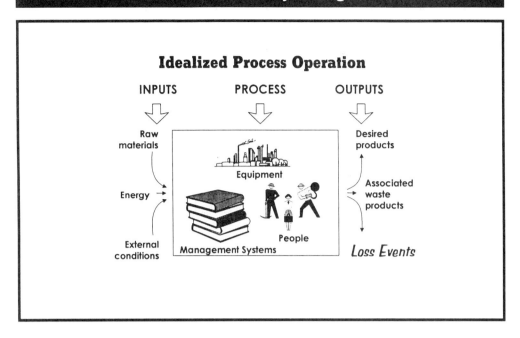

The diagram above represents an idealized process operation. All businesses share these elements in different ways. A refinery may have a huge capital investment in equipment, whereas a retail store has a significant amount of retail sales products. A travel agent may only have a computer and phone and little else in the way of equipment. All systems have people in them. Their goal is to produce the greatest amount of desired product while minimizing the waste products and eliminating loss events.

Management systems are developed by the organization to control how the people interact with the equipment and with each other. Typical management systems include equipment design process, equipment maintenance, procedures, training, receipt control, warehousing practices, and employment screening processes.

Through proper design and implementation of these management systems, we can prevent loss events from occurring.

Loss Event

- Any action, state, or condition in which a system is not meeting one or more of its design intents
    - inability to continuously fulfill a function over a period of time (unreliability)
    - inability to provide a function at a specified time (unavailability)
    - too much downtime over a period of time (high average unavailability)
    - too many failures over a period of time (high rate of failure)
    - too much time to restore system or component function (poor maintainability)
- Includes actual losses and near misses

Characteristics of Loss Events

- Are unplanned
- Involve a combination of human errors, equipment failures, and/or external events
- Have significant impacts on economics, safety/health, and the environment
- Generally have underlying root causes that create error-likely situations for people and vulnerabilities for equipment
- Frequently preceded by identifiable precursors that can be detected and corrected
- Will always be possible, but can be effectively managed

Effects of Loss Events

- Less capability
  - inherent capability limitations
  - capability degradation
- Less output
  - quality of products
  - unplanned outages
  - planned outages
- Inefficiency
  - human resource consumption
  - material consumption
  - equipment consumption
  - utility consumption
- Increased liability risk
  - business
  - safety/health
  - environmental

Simple Scenario Producing a Loss Event

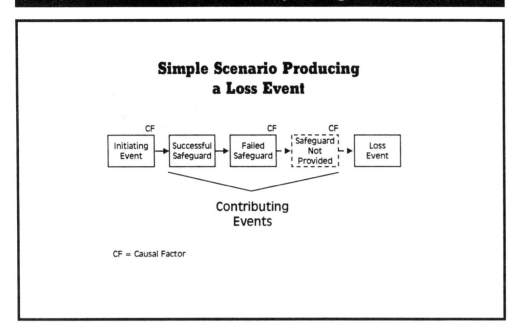

CF = Causal Factor

Initiating Event

An initiating event is an event in a scenario that, if unmitigated, causes one or more loss events to occur

Contributing Events

Successful safeguards

Successful safeguards are events in a scenario that represent successful execution of planned actions for preventing/mitigating potential losses associated with initiating events

Failed safeguards

Failed safeguards are events in a scenario that represent unsuccessful execution of planned actions for preventing/mitigating potential losses associated with initiating events

Safeguards not provided

These are events that do not appear in a scenario, but could (or should) have been provided as planned actions for preventing/mitigating potential losses associated with initiating events

Causal factors

- Key human errors or equipment failures that, if eliminated, would have prevented a loss event or reduced its effects
- Typical causal factors:
    - initiating event
    - each failed safeguard
    - each reasonable safeguard that was not provided

More Complex Scenario Producing a Loss Event

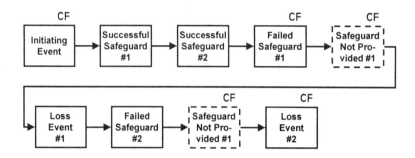

CF = Causal Factor

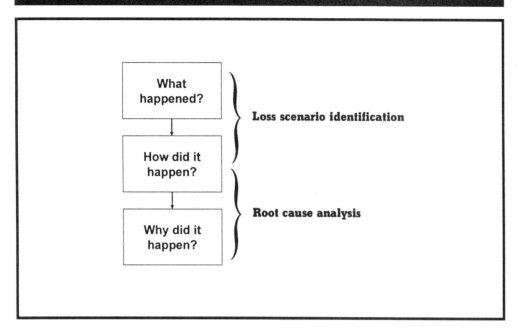

Understanding the Loss Scenario Is Not Enough

- Scenarios tell us what happened, not why it happened
- Events in loss scenarios are generally only symptoms of underlying problems in the administrative controls that are supposed to keep those events from occurring
- Understanding only the scenario can address the outward symptoms, but not the underlying problems
- More investigation of the underlying problems is needed to find and correct underlying problems that will contribute to future loss events

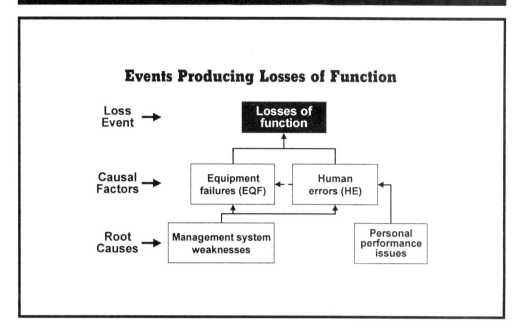

Events Producing Losses of Function

Root Cause Definition

- The most basic causes of an event that
  - can be reasonably identified, and
  - management has control/influence to fix
- Typically, root causes are the absence, neglect, or deficiencies of management systems that control human actions and equipment performance

This diagram illustrates how management system weaknesses lead to human errors, equipment failures, and external events that produce loss events. Note that each management system weakness may influence more than one human error, equipment failure, or external event.

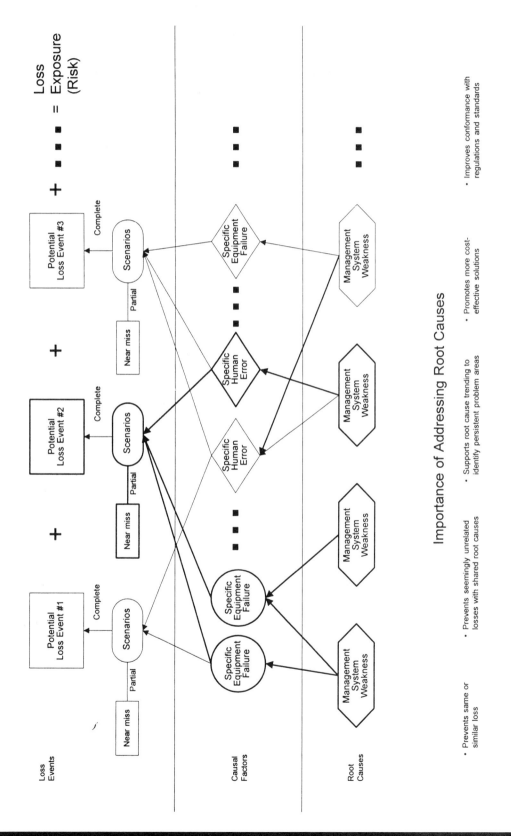

Features of Root Cause Analysis

- Provides an understanding of how a loss event occurred
- Helps discover the underlying root causes (management system weaknesses) of the key contributors (causal factors)
- Helps in developing/implementing practical and effective recommendations for preventing future losses

Key Differences from Traditional Problem Solving

- Logic reasoning through cause-effect relationships
  - This ensures that our solutions address the real causes of the events.
- Rigorous focus on factual data versus supposition
  - The problem can't be solved until data concerning the event are gathered and analyzed.
- Range of possibilities considered
  - Often the first, most obvious cause is not the real cause of the event. The real cause remains hidden because the analyst doesn't consider other possibilities.
- Management system perspective
  - Management system weaknesses are the real root causes of events. By changing the way things are done, future events are prevented.
- Multiple root causes identified
  - Events always have more than one cause. All of the causes should be identified and corrected. The identification of "the" cause of the events is impossible.
- Systematic processes/tools make effective data trending possible
  - Unless consistent methods are used to analyze and document events, trending is not possible. Trending is useful for identifying recurring problems and issues.

This flowchart (modeled after AIChE's process for conducting incident investigations) illustrates the complete process of performing root cause analyses.

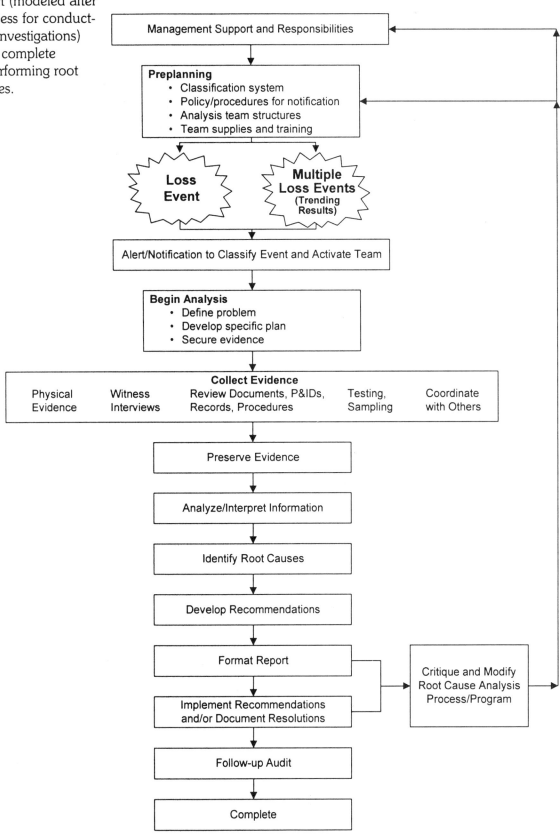

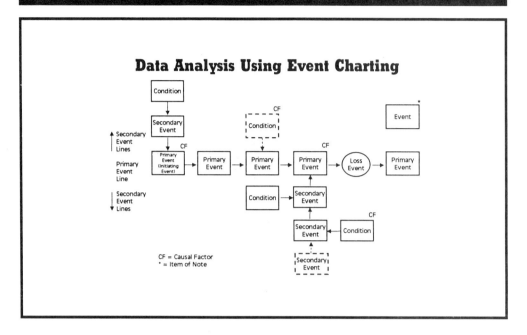

Data Analysis Using Event Charting

As the data are collected, they need to be analyzed. Two useful techniques for data analysis are event charting and the 5 Whys technique

Event Charting

Event charting is a written or graphical description for the time sequence of contributing events associated with an incident

Purposes

- Identifies contributing events available from data gathering
- Differentiates unconfirmed assumptions from verified events (facts)
- Stimulates and guides additional data-gathering activities by identifying gaps in known information
- Provides an overview of the accident process
- Establishes the relative timing of events and sets the time frame of interest for the incident
- Focuses attention on key systems associated with contributing events
- In some cases, the accident chronology can simply be expanded in sufficient detail to expose root causes without the need for more intensive logic models

Example Results

Example — Causal Factor Diagram

Transducer for V-23 failed
~8:50 p.m.

CF V-23 failed closed
~8:50 p.m.

Pump running deadheaded

Fragrance level in production areas reduced

Sample frequency reduced to 1/24 hours at noon

No sampling of material is performed during event

Fragrance flow stopped
~8:50 p.m.

Product was off-specification

CF Operators do not realize the significance of the loss of fragrance smell

No trouble-shooting guidelines exist for this system

Ray thought dirt/grease on the pump motor caused the overheating

CF Operators failed to identify the cause of the shutdown

P-10 shuts down from overheating

Production line shuts down
10:07 p.m.

Valve position on control panel shows demand position, not actual position

All control panel indications were normal

No local flow indications were provided

CF Operators failed to detect V-23 still closed

Emma/Ray cleaned pump motor

Pump returned to service
~10:50 p.m.

Production line restarted
11:30 p.m.

V-23 still failed closed

No sampling of product performed during event

No trouble-shooting guidelines for this system

Jack and Chris discover failed transducer on V-23
2:50 a.m.

Pump running deadheaded

P-10 shuts down
12:48 a.m.

Production line shuts down a second time
12:48 a.m.

CF Trouble-shooting of problem takes ~2 hours
12:55 a.m. – 2:50 a.m.

Jack and Chris begin troubleshooting problem
12:55 a.m.

Chris is not trained on this specific type of transducer

Chris begins repair of pump
2:50 a.m.

Chris completes repair of pump
3:15 a.m.

Repair of transducer takes 25 minutes
2:50 a.m. – 3:15 a.m.

Off-specification product was rerun

$250,000 lost in production and off-specification product

Item of Note: PMs for the control loop had been overlooked twice

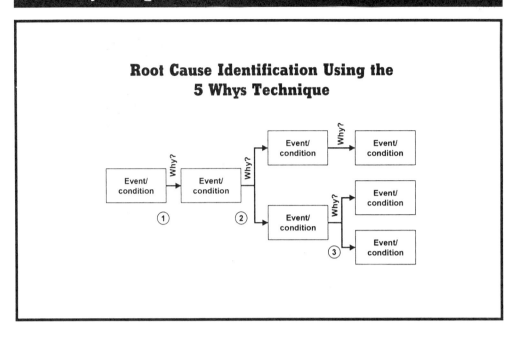

Root Cause Identification Using the 5 Whys Technique

The 5 Whys Technique

The 5 Whys technique is a brainstorming-type technique for analyzing data and identifying root causes of incidents through questioning *why* events occurred or conditions existed.

Using the 5 Whys

- Start with a loss or select one event associated with an incident
- Ask why this event occurred (i.e., the most direct cause of the event)
- Solicit answer(s) to this question (the answer may identify more than one sub-event or condition as cause)
- For each of these sub-events or causes, ask why it occurred
- Solicit answers to these why questions and repeat the process through at least three more iterations of why questions
- Repeat the process for the other events associated with the incident

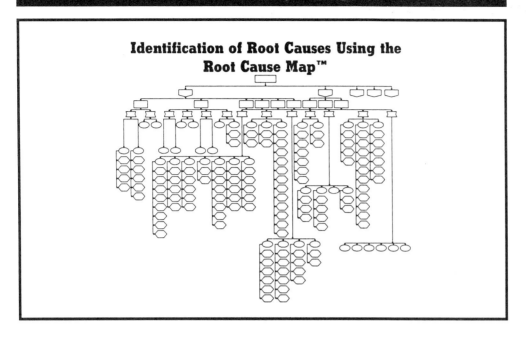

Identification of Root Causes Using the Root Cause Map™

Using the Root Cause Map™

- Identify causal factors (using an event chart or the 5 Whys). Remember, causal factors are the key human errors and equipment failures that led to the loss event or made it more severe.
- Work through the map for each causal factor
- Step down the root path, noting:
  - primary difficulty source (equipment, personnel, other)
  - problem category
  - major root cause category
  - near root cause
  - root cause
- Record results on forms, at each step
- Perform 5 Whys if root causes are not deep enough
- Use root causes (and perhaps categories) for:
  - generating recommendations
  - trending

> A copy of the Root Cause Map™ is inserted in this book

Advantages to using the map

- Ease of use
  - The Root Cause Map™ provides a quick and easy-to-learn method for performing root cause analysis.
- Consistency
  - By providing a checklist in the form of a tree structure, different analysts can consistently identify root causes for events. This enables meaningful trending to be performed.
- Easy to document
  - Because a common framework is used for performing root cause analysis, the process can be automated to speed the documentation process.

Example Root Cause Summary Table

Causal Factor	Paths Through Root Cause Map™	Recommendations
The operator failed to close the inlet valve on Tank C. **Background** The operator was transferring acid from the acid make-up tank to Tank B. The step in the procedure said "Verify that there is sufficient acid in the make-up tank. If not, make up acid. Turn on agitator on acid make-up tank, and agitate for 10 minutes. Close the inlet valve on Tank A. Close the inlet valve on Tank C. Close the inlet valve on Tank B." The operator completed all of the steps except to close the inlet valve on Tank C.	• Personnel difficulty • Company employee • Procedures • Misleading/confusing • More than one action per step The procedure contains numerous actions in one step. • Personnel difficulty • Company employee • Procedures • Misleading/confusing • Format confusing or LTA* The procedure is written in paragraph format. It should be written in a more user-friendly format.	Revise the procedure so that the instructions are divided into discrete steps. Provide a checkoff for discrete steps. (Procedures Group, Operations Department) Include a section in the facility procedure reviews that requires the reviewer to ensure that instructions are divided into discrete steps with a checkoff or data entry blank for each step. (Procedures Group, Operations Department)

* Less than adequate

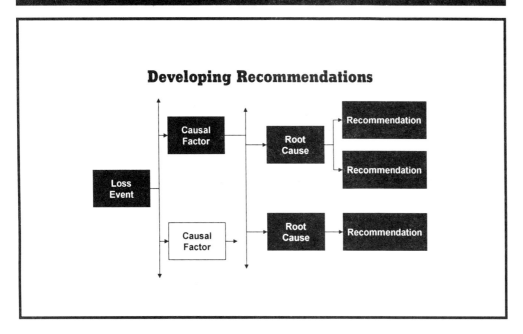

Developing Recommendations

Key Recommendation Concepts

- Recommendations are the most important products of analyses
- Recommendations should address system improvements aimed at a problem's root cause(s)
- Recommendations should inhibit the flow of events

Successful recommendations

- Address options for reducing frequency, minimizing exposures, and/or lessening the consequences of one or more root causes
- Clearly state the intended action
- Are practical, feasible, and achievable
- Increase the number of events necessary to generate a loss event
- Do not pose other undesirable and/or unforeseen risks
- Are compatible with other objectives of the system/plant
- Are based on conclusions from data analysis results
- Have assigned responsibility and a date for completion

Typically there are three categories of recommendations

1. Correct the specific problem discovered through this investigation
2. Correct other similar problems that currently exist
3. Correct the process that creates these problems

Example — Procedure step to close six valves does not include all of the valves (it only includes five of six valves).

1. Specific — Revise procedure X-547 to include valve XT-272

2. Similar problems — Review procedures used in the off-loading process to ensure all required actions are included in the procedures

3. Correct the process — Revise the procedure generation process to include a walkthrough of the procedure in the field

Suggested format for recommendations

- Provide a general objective to be accomplished, followed by a specific example of how it could be accomplished. This ensures that the recommendation is clearly described, yet allows flexibility in meeting the general objective.

Example — Provide a means for operators to detect slow changes in tank levels. For example, a strip chart recorder that shows trends over 8 hours could be provided.

Chapter 6

Reliability Management Programs

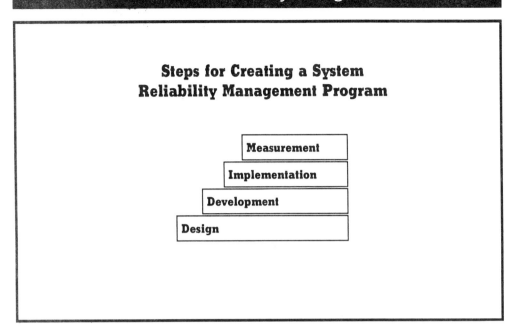

Steps for Creating a System Reliability Management Program

There are four fundamental steps to creating a system reliability management program:

Design

The design step establishes the specification of the system reliability program. This specification defines what must be done, not necessarily how it will be done.

Development

The development step produces a management system (including associated guidelines, procedures, training modules, etc.) to satisfy the design specification. The product of the development stage becomes the guide for implementation of the program.

Implementation

The implementation step brings the plans described in the program description into reality.

Measurement

The measurement step defines key performance indicators to be used to evaluate the performance of the program to make necessary improvements.

Key Aspects of Program Design

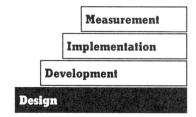

- Purpose
- Scope
- Goals
- Roles/responsibilities
- Training requirements
- Documentation requirements

Key Aspects of Program Design

Program description/purpose

Define the purpose of establishing a system reliability program and the overall objective of the program.

Scope

Identify those items to be included in the system reliability program. Consider expanding the scope beyond equipment and hardware to all areas within the organization (e.g., quality control, operations, product distribution, training, procedures).

System reliability goals

Establish specific qualitative and quantitative goals to provide a means of measuring progress and to identify areas in which improvement is needed.

Roles/responsibilities

Identify specific job titles/positions that are to play an active role in system reliability implementation activities. Define the responsibilities of these individuals and the level of authority of each.

Training requirements

Determine the training requirements necessary for those team members who will play an active role in the system reliability program. Equip team members with the knowledge necessary to meet the program goals.

Documentation requirements

Define the documentation requirements necessary for program implementation and for historical reference purposes.

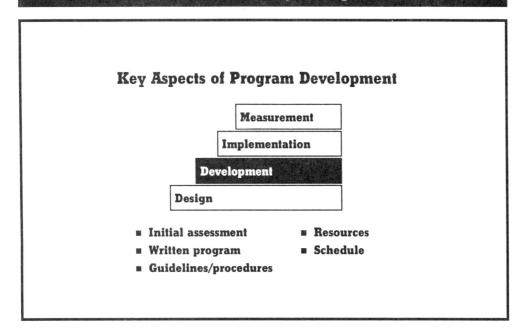

Key Aspects of Program Development

Initial assessment

Perform a corporate and facility survey to identify current system reliability activities. Conduct a detailed assessment of the activities and define gaps in the existing system reliability program.

Written program

Document the philosophical approach taken in establishing the system reliability program and include an account for influence by other quality standards (ANSI/ISO/ASQC 9000 programs, etc.). Identify (1) those specific activities that must take place to fulfill program requirements and (2) those responsible for performing such activities.

Guidelines/procedures

Establish a company protocol for performing various implementation tasks.

Resources

Allocate sufficient resources (e.g., time, people, funding) for performing program tasks to meet system reliability goals.

Schedule

Develop and distribute a schedule for implementing program activities and for reaching system reliability goals. Determine long lead-time activities and critical path activities. Allow team members to review the schedule in order to obtain team "buy-in."

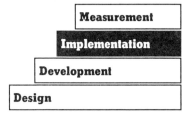

Key Aspects of Program Implementation

- Communication
- Task assignment
- Training
- Tools

Key Aspects of Program Implementation

Communication

Communicate the purpose, scope, and goals of the system reliability program to all affected employees. Inform team members of those specific tasks that must be implemented in order to fulfill the purposes of the program. Solicit suggestions from team members for improving the program.

Task assignment

Assign implementation tasks to responsible parties, fully communicating performance expectations and schedule requirements.

Training

Provide associated training for performing system reliability activities. Ensure that the content of the training is appropriate and verify that students understand the training.

Tools

Provide the necessary tools for performing system reliability activities.

Key Aspects of Program Measurement

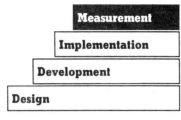

- Performance indicators
- Audits
- Data trending

Key Aspects of Program Measurement

Performance indicators

Define direct and indirect performance indicators and targets.

Audits

Establish a system reliability auditing protocol. Perform periodic audits and assess facility compliance with company reliability policy.

Data trending

Use data trending to identify system reliability program problems.

Further Information

If you have questions or comments on the material presented in this document, please contact EQE International, Inc. at:

> EQE International, Inc.
> 1000 Technology Drive
> Knoxville, TN 37932-3353
> Phone: (865) 966-5232
> Fax: (865) 966-5287
> E-mail: sri@jbfa.com
> On the web at: http://www.jbfa.com

Government Institutes Mini-Catalog

PC #	ENVIRONMENTAL TITLES	Pub Date	Price
629	ABCs of Environmental Regulation: Understanding the Fed Regs	1998	$49
627	ABCs of Environmental Science	1998	$39
672	Book of Lists for Regulated Hazardous Substances, 9th Edition	1999	$79
579	Brownfields Redevelopment	1998	$79
4100	CFR Chemical Lists on CD ROM, 1998 Edition	1997	$125
4089	Chemical Data for Workplace Sampling & Analysis, Single User Disk	1997	$125
512	Clean Water Handbook, 2nd Edition	1996	$89
581	EH&S Auditing Made Easy	1997	$79
673	E H & S CFR Training Requirements, 4th Edition	1999	$89
4082	EMMI-Envl Monitoring Methods Index for Windows-Network	1997	$537
4082	EMMI-Envl Monitoring Methods Index for Windows-Single User	1997	$179
525	Environmental Audits, 7th Edition	1996	$79
548	Environmental Engineering and Science: An Introduction	1997	$79
643	Environmental Guide to the Internet, 4rd Edition	1998	$59
650	Environmental Law Handbook, 15th Edition	1999	$89
353	Environmental Regulatory Glossary, 6th Edition	1993	$79
652	Environmental Statutes, 1999 Edition	1999	$79
4097	OSHA CFRs Made Easy (29 CFRs)/CD ROM	1998	$129
4102	1999 Title 21 Food & Drug CFRs on CD ROM-Single User	1999	$325
4099	Environmental Statutes on CD ROM for Windows-Single User	1999	$139
570	Environmentalism at the Crossroads	1995	$39
536	ESAs Made Easy	1996	$59
515	Industrial Environmental Management: A Practical Approach	1996	$79
510	ISO 14000: Understanding Environmental Standards	1996	$69
551	ISO 14001: An Executive Report	1996	$55
588	International Environmental Auditing	1998	$149
518	Lead Regulation Handbook	1996	$79
554	Property Rights: Understanding Government Takings	1997	$79
582	Recycling & Waste Mgmt Guide to the Internet	1997	$49
615	Risk Management Planning Handbook	1998	$89
603	Superfund Manual, 6th Edition	1997	$115
566	TSCA Handbook, 3rd Edition	1997	$95
534	Wetland Mitigation: Mitigation Banking and Other Strategies	1997	$75

PC #	SAFETY and HEALTH TITLES	Pub Date	Price
547	Construction Safety Handbook	1996	$79
553	Cumulative Trauma Disorders	1997	$59
663	Forklift Safety, 2nd Edition	1999	$69
539	Fundamentals of Occupational Safety & Health	1996	$49
612	HAZWOPER Incident Command	1998	$59
535	Making Sense of OSHA Compliance	1997	$59
589	Managing Fatigue in Transportation, *ATA Conference*	1997	$75
558	PPE Made Easy	1998	$79
598	Project Mgmt for E H & S Professionals	1997	$59
552	Safety & Health in Agriculture, Forestry and Fisheries	1997	$125
669	Safety & Health on the Internet, 4th Edition	1999	$59
597	Safety Is A People Business	1997	$49
668	Safety Made Easy, 2nd	1999	$59
590	Your Company Safety and Health Manual	1997	$79

Government Institutes
4 Research Place, Suite 200 • Rockville, MD 20850-3226
Tel. (301) 921-2323 • FAX (301) 921-0264
Email: giinfo@govinst.com • Internet: http://www.govinst.com

Please call our customer service department at (301) 921-2323 for a free publications catalog.

CFRs now available online. Call (301) 921-2355 for info.

Government Institutes Order Form

4 Research Place, Suite 200 • Rockville, MD 20850-3226
Tel (301) 921-2323 • Fax (301) 921-0264
Internet: http://www.govinst.com • E-mail: giinfo@govinst.com

4 EASY WAYS TO ORDER

1. Tel: **(301) 921-2323**
Have your credit card ready when you call.

2. Fax: **(301) 921-0264**
Fax this completed order form with your company purchase order or credit card information.

3. Mail: **Government Institutes Division**
ABS Group Inc.
P.O. Box 846304
Dallas, TX 75284-6304 USA

Mail this completed order form with a check, company purchase order, or credit card information.

4. Online: Visit http://www.govinst.com

PAYMENT OPTIONS

❑ **Check** *(payable in US dollars to ABS Group Inc. Government Institutes Division)*

❑ **Purchase Order** *(This order form must be attached to your company P.O. Note: All International orders must be prepaid.)*

❑ **Credit Card** ❑ VISA ❑ MasterCard ❑ American Express

Exp. ___ /____

Credit Card No. _____

Signature _____

(Government Institutes' Federal I.D.# is 13-2695912)

CUSTOMER INFORMATION

Ship To: (Please attach your purchase order)

Name _____

GI Account # (7 digits on mailing label) _____

Company/Institution _____

Address _____
(Please supply street address for UPS shipping)

City _____ State/Province _____

Zip/Postal Code _____ Country _____

Tel ( ) _____

Fax ( ) _____

Email Address _____

Bill To: (if different from ship-to address)

Name _____

Title/Position _____

Company/Institution _____

Address _____
(Please supply street address for UPS shipping)

City _____ State/Province _____

Zip/Postal Code _____ Country _____

Tel ( ) _____

Fax ( ) _____

Email Address _____

Qty.	Product Code	Title	Price

❑ **New Edition No Obligation Standing Order Program**
Please enroll me in this program for the products I have ordered. Government Institutes will notify me of new editions by sending me an invoice. I understand that there is no obligation to purchase the product. This invoice is simply my reminder that a new edition has been released.

15 DAY MONEY-BACK GUARANTEE
If you're not completely satisfied with any product, return it undamaged within 15 days for a full and immediate refund on the price of the product.

SOURCE CODE: BP01

Subtotal _____
MD Residents add 5% Sales Tax _____
Shipping and Handling (see box below) _____
Total Payment Enclosed _____

Shipping and Handling	**Sales Tax**
Within U.S:	Maryland 5%
1-4 products: $6/product	Tennessee 6%
5 or more: $4/product	Texas 8.25%
Outside U.S:	Virginia 4.5%
Add $15 for each item (Global)	